D1564999

Gloriosiss
Roberti
Bellarmini
S.R.E.
Presbyteri
Cardinalis
Archiepisc.
Capu.

DE CONTROVERSIIS FIDEI CHRISTIANI

# DE ECCLESIA MILITANTE
### DIFFUSA PER ORBEM TERRARIUM

✠

# ON THE CHURCH MILITANT
### DIFFUSED THROUGHOUT THE WORLD

by
ST. ROBERT BELLARMINE, S.J.
*Doctor of the Church*

Translated from the original Latin by:
Ryan Grant

MEDIATRIX PRESS

ISBN: 978-0692736760

Translated from *De Controversiis Fidei Christiani, contra haereticos nostri tempori, tomus primus, De Ecclesia,* lib. 3.
Prague, 1721
2nd Edition.

Mediatrix Press
607 E. 6th Ave.
Post Falls, ID 83854
www.mediatrixpress.com

# TABLE OF CONTENTS

## MICHAEL G. SIRILLA, Ph.D.
### Franciscan University of Steubenville

S T. ROBERT BELLARMINE (1542–1621), a preeminent and officially-recognized Doctor of the Church, is the most important figure in the Catholic Counter-Reformation. His prodigious works have been received for centuries as standard and decisive for the promotion and defense of the truth of Christ's revelations on justification, the sacraments, the four last things (eschatology), and Christian spirituality. Even more importantly, his theological writings on the Church of Christ constitute an invaluable treasure not only for Catholics, but for the commonweal and eternal salvation of humanity itself. This is no slight exaggeration. His is the very first independent theological and dogmatic treatise on the Church. Patristic and medieval Catholic authors treated on the mystery of the Church, to be sure; but they provided no free-standing treatment *de ecclesia*. Bellarmine's is the first and the best of its kind. And yet, his writings–mostly composed in Latin–have remained largely unavailable to the English-speaking world until several years ago, when Mr. Ryan Grant began publishing superbly readable translations of the works of this great doctor. But why were Bellarmine's works available only in Latin for so many years?

There are two principal reasons for this. The first is that the theologians who needed to access them were scholars who had a command of the Latin language—something standard for Catholic theologians at least until the mid-1960s. For example, up to this time the final examinations for the licentiate and doctoral degrees in both philosophy and theology in the Church were administered orally and in Latin. And, of course, it is much better to read the writings of your primary sources in their original language instead of depending on the work of a translator. The second reason is more political and ideological in nature. St. Bellarmine, being the most prominent Catholic intellectual behind the counter-reformation, was viewed just before, during, and most certainly after Vatican II, as the prime example of the rigid, self-enclosed, anti-ecumenical, and anti-modern thinker that those inebriated with the ersatz spirit of Vatican II wanted to eschew. Those possessed of this mentality relegated Bellarmine and all early modern Catholic thinkers (and this includes the countless other venerable doctors such as Ligouri, De Sales, Suarez, Melchior Cano, among others) to the dust heap of Catholic history as "ghettoizing" throwbacks who foolishly clung to an untenable form of Catholic life and thought made irrelevant by the modern political and religious revolutions.

And yet these claims cannot stand. In fact, the Second Vatican Council itself vindicates St. Bellarmine's definition of the Church militant (the Church on earth) in article 14 of the "Dogmatic Constitution on the Church" where we read, "The bonds which bind men to the Church in a visible way are the profession of faith, the sacraments, and ecclesiastical government and communion." This is essentially how St. Bellarmine defines the Church on earth with in "De Ecclesia Militante," book 3, chapter 2, as translated by Mr. Grant: The Church is "that one and true ... body of men of the same Christian profession and of the same Sacraments gathered in communion, under the rule of legitimate pastors and especially of the one Vicar of Christ on Earth, the Roman Pontiff." Thus, the current English translation of Bellarmine's *De Ecclesia* is of inestimable value for those English-speaking students of Catholic theology who wish not only to understand properly the essence of the ecclesiology of Vatican II, but the official magisterial teaching of the Church on Her essence and mission as the sole institution established by our Lord for the salvation of souls and the glory of God.

On a personal note, for over a decade I have had to provide my ecclesiology students with my own translations of select portions of St. Robert Bellarmine's treatise on the Church. With this and his other translations of St. Bellarmine's works on the Church, Mr. Grant has provided an unmatched service to the English-speaking world of Catholic theologians and students of theology. I strongly recommend this volume, along with his others in this series, as a principal text for teachers and students of Catholic ecclesiology. Mr. Grant's translation is precise and consummately readable. Let us look forward with hope to his further translation projects.

Steubenville, Ohio
June 6, 2016
Feast of St. Norbert

THIS particular book, *On the Church Militant* has been excerpted from Bellarmine's treatise on the Church in general, which begins with a treatise on Councils, followed by this work and then by *On the Marks of the Church*, which was published in January of 2015. What is particularly important here, is that Bellarmine lays down principles that become the fundamental principles of ecclesiology. Then in future books on the Church, such as his work on Clergy, Monks and Laity, all the particular considerations follow logically from the principles laid out here.

Those familiar with my translations *On the Marks of the Church*, and *On the Roman Pontiff*, will be familiar with Bellarmine's style and the general *mores* of books in the 16th century. The original has no footnotes and sources are in the text as part of the writing. These I have re-written as footnotes to clean up the readability of the text. I have left the references as they appear in the text. It is important to note that some of the references may have shifted in their numbering since Bellarmine's time, or in attribution.

A word is in order about Scripture, the Fathers and the Protestants whom Bellarmine quotes. Bellarmine had most of the Bible completely memorized, from an edition that did not have versification. Sometimes, subsequent to his time, certain verses in Scripture were rendered differently. If this has occurred, I translate what Bellarmine has and note the variation in the footnote. Secondly, where Scripture is concerned, I have made my own translations from the Vulgate, rather than using translations based on the Vulgate.. This is because it is important to understand the Vulgate as Bellarmine did, not as Englishmen half a world away that rendered it for an entirely different purpose. In like manner, I have also rendered the Fathers and other authors, e.g. Calvin, from their Latin works. With Calvin this is particularly because I have not found any translations of the *Institutes* coming from the French satisfactory, so I have consulted the 1559 Latin version which seems to be the one Bellarmine used in his own citations, and consequently this is important because it again shows us how Bellarmine understood Calvin.

It is also important to understand the style of argumentation. For Bellarmine argumentation is made from Scripture and also from the Church Fathers. Though Bellarmine certainly agreed that individual Fathers could err or go astray, nevertheless, following the principles of all theologians and the Council of Trent, if they were found in a common consensus then the teaching must be infallible. Thus the copious citations of the Fathers which make up this work are necessary to draw a consensus on given points of argument.

Next, I would like to especially thank all of those who made this work possible, firstly my wife, whose patience and great sacrifices have allowed me to get this completed, as well as those who assisted me financially in the production of this work, especially Eric and Katy Mack, Fr. David Hust, and many others whose generous donations made it possible, for the glory of Jesus and Mary.


Post Falls ID
3 June 2016
Feast of the Sacred Heart of Jesus

## DEDICATIO

Omnibus benefactoribus laboris S. Roberti Bellarmini votum esse, et praesertim Erico et Kætalynæ Mack, praesidio ejus remoto, hic liber fieri non posset.

Dedicated to all the benefactors of the St. Robert Bellarmine project, and most especially Eric and Katy Mack, without whose assistance this work would not be possible.

# CHAPTER I
## *On the term "Church"*

THE CONTROVERSY on the Church Militant has many parts. In the first place, what the Church itself is must be argued, and then on the members, that is, clergy, monks and laity. Again, the Church Militant must be considered according to what it is, and this is what we now hasten to dispute. There are three particular controversies: 1) On the term "Church" and its definition; 2) On the quality or the visibility of the Church; 3) On the marks whereby it can be known for certain.

We now commence with the first, but before we get too far into it we ought to note those who have written about the Church, or rather, whose books we have read since we have not read everything. So, the following authors have written on this point about the Church: St. Augustine;[1] St. Cyprian;[2] Optatus;[3] and from more recent authors who have written on this matter we have Thomas

---

[1] *De Unitate Ecclesiae.*

[2] *De Unitate Ecclesiae.*

[3] *Contra Parmenianum,* in six books.

1

Waldens;[4] Juan Torquemada;[5] John Driedo;[6] Albert Pighius;[7] Cardinal Hosius in his confession, as well as in his explication of the Creed, and his *Contra prolegomena Brentii*, lib. 5; Pedro de Soto;[8] John of Daventria;[9] John Cochlaeus,[10] Johan Eck;[11] Alonso de Castro;[12] John of Louvain;[13] Francis Turrianus[14] and Melchior Cano.[15] After these, in the beginning of the year 1577, we disputed this very treatise (which we are now publishing) in the schools, and in that time Gregory of Valentia also wrote on the same issue[16] and others also wrote, but he was not free from other occupations to explain their books.

---

[4] Lib. 2. *doctrin. fid.* cap. 8.9.10, etc.

[5] *Summam de Ecclesia.*

[6] in lib. 4 de dogm. Ecclesiast., cap. 2.

[7] *Controversia*, 3.

[8] 1 parte defensionis suae contra Brentium.

[9] in confut. 7 artic. Confessionis Augustanae.

[10] Philippica 4, et in lib. de Scripturae et Ecclesiae Auctoritrate.

[11] *Enchiridium.*

[12] lib. 6 contra haeres.

[13] In explicat. Symboli and all others who have written on the Creed.

[14] In two books de Ecclesia et ordinat. Ministr.

[15] *de Locis*, lib. 4.

[16] In his *Analysis fidei Catholicae*, parte 6.

ON THE TERM "CHURCH"

I come now to the proposed disputation, which is on the first point, the term "Church". The name is Greek and is deduced from the word åêêáëŸþ, (*ekkaleô*), which means *I call out*. Therefore, Church is an evocation, or a body of those called out. Moreover, the people of God is a body of those called out, because no man joins himself to this people by himself and by his own instinct, but any whosoever that come have been preceded by the calling of God. For the calling is the first benefit, which the saints receive from God, as the Apostle says in Romans, "He called them and justified them, and glorified those whom he had justified."[17] The Apostle says often enough that Christians are called, in fact in nearly every epistle.

Moreover, three things must be noted on this term. 1) The name of Church can be joined with another thing, and can be received on the side of the good and the bad. For the Psalms speak of the "Church of the malignant,"[18] and "the Church of the Saints".[19] Moreover, this term is placed absolutely, it is not understood unless it is about the Church of Christ, with the exception of one passage, that is Acts 19 where it says about the people of the heathen "For the Church was confused."

2) Mark with St. Augustine, "God stood in the synagogue of the gods,"[20] although the Church of the Old

---

[17] Romans 8:30.

[18] Psal. 25(26).

[19] Psalm. 88 (89).

[20] *In Psal. 81 (82).*

3

Testament and the New are the same, nevertheless the state of the new Testament Church is by far more excellent, thus, the names are also distinct, for the people of the Old Testament are properly called the Synagogue, that is the congregation; but the people of the New Testament is never called the Synagogue, but always the Church, that is the evocation. To be gathered is common among both men and beasts, but to be called out is proper to men. It is not related that the people of the Jews in the Old Testament are also everywhere called the Church; for both the Synagogue and the Church are called in Hebrew by the word "congregation" חדע, [e-dah] which we translate into Synagogue, and is said to be from דעי [ya-ad] "to assign or gather". Likewise, לחק [qa-hal] that is "the Church," is said to come from from להק, "to gather". Therefore there are two names, but they mean altogether the same thing.

3) It also must be noted that in the same way as the city on the one hand means a body of men, on the other the place in which that body lives, so also the Church in the Scriptures means the body of the faithful, as it says in Romans 16: "All the Churches of Asia greet you." Now, all the faithful are gathered in that very citation, just as in Judith 6: "every people prayed through the whole night within the Church," although we now only mean the body of the faithful when we dispute on the Church.

## CHAPTER II
### *On the Definition of the Church*

HERE are five heretical opinions on the definition of the Church. The first is that the Church is the congregation of the predestined, so that only all those who have been predestined would constitute the Church. This is the opinion of John Wycliffe[1] and Jan Hus whose position is contained in a condemnation by the Council of Constance: "A man foreknown, although he might be in grace for a time according to the present justice, is still never part of the Holy Church whereas a man predestined will always remain a member of the Church, although at some time he may fall from the grace he has attained thus far, still not from the grace of predestination.[2]

The second is that the Church would be a multitude of perfect men having no sin. Certain Pelgians taught this, as St. Augustine relates where he says: "To it also come the Pelagians, in order to say that the life of the just in this world is entirely free from sin, and that the Church of Christ is formed of men of this kind in this mortal life."[3]

---

[1] Quoted in Waldens, tom. 1, lib. 2, cap. 8.

[2] Artic. 1,2, 3, 5, 6 as is contained in the Council of Constance, sess. 15.

[3] *De haeresibus,* ca. 88.

Calvin attributes the same teaching to the Anabaptists of this time.[4]

The third is that the Church might be a congregation of the just, or better still those who have never failed to make the confession of faith. This is distinguished from the second opinion in that it excluded each and every sinner, but this does not exclude anyone except notable sinners. Formerly, St. Cyprian thought Novation was the author of this opinion,[5] and Augustine the Donatists,[6] for I believe Calvin and others were deceived who thought that the followers of Novation and the Donatists excluded every kind of sinner. For, Cyprian and Epiphanius clearly say that they retained swindlers, adulterers and the like in the Church but only excluded those who had lapsed under persecution.[7] Moreover, what Ambrose[8] and Theodoret[9] say does not appear opposed to this, that the Novationists abolished the power of forgiving all sins, save for the lightest. For even if they did not absolve grave sinners they still retained them in their body unless they lapsed in the confession of faith. Augustine also teaches[10] that the Donatists did not abhor all sins, but only certain greater

---

[4] *Instit.*, lib. 4, cap. 1, §13.

[5] Lib. 1, epist. 2

[6] lib. *De Haeres.* cap. 69.

[7] Cyprian lib. 4, epist. 2; Epiphanius *in haeres. Catharorum.*

[8] lib. 1 *de poenitentia*, cap. 1-2.

[9] lib. 3 *de fabulis haereticorum.*

[10] *Contra Parmenianum*, lib. 3, cap. 2.

crimes; one that they objected to is that they thought Catholics were traitors to the divine books.

The fourth is of the Confessionists, who, although they condemn the Pelagians, Novationists and Donatists by name, still their opinion is a composite of those heresies. For: 1) Not only the Confessionists, but all Lutherans and Calvinists teach that there is no sin that is venial by nature, rather, all are in and of themselves mortal, but venial by the mercy of God, who does not impute these to believers. Luther teaches this[11] as well as Melanchthon[12] and Calvin.[13]

2) The Augsburg Confession, in article 7, teaches that the Church is the congregation of the Saints who truly believe and obey God. And Melanchthon, in his defense of it, tries to show that sinners do not pertain to the Church except in name. John Brenz teaches similar things in the Prolegomena against Pedro de Soto. Nor is it opposed that Melanchthon and Brenz both say that the wicked are mixed with the good, for they in effect create two Churches. One that is true, and to which the privileges related in the Scriptures pertain; this is the congregation of the Saints who truly believe and obey God, and this one is not visible but can only be seen with the eyes of faith. The other is external, which is a Church in name only, and this is the congregation of men coming together in the

---

[11] *in assert.* art. 32.

[12] *In locis* cap. de discrimine peccati mortalis et venialis.

[13] *Instit.* lib. 2, cap. 8, §58 et 59.

doctrine of faith, and the use of the sacraments; in this the good and bad are discovered. Consequently, they never mean that the wicked are parts of the true Church and so Melanchthon cautiously does not say the Church consists from the wicked as well as the good, but says the wicked are mixed into the Church. Moreover, Brenz says that the wicked are in the Church in some manner, but they are not of the Church.

Luther in his work *de Conciliis et Ecclesia*, in the third part, says that the Church is the holy Christian people. That he might show himself to speak on the sanctity of each of the members, he tries to show the Pope and Cardinals are not of the Church because they are not holy. Therefore, if only the just are part of the true Church, and all sins, in so far as they are light, are mortal sins and make a man unjust; it follows that only the perfect and those lacking all sin are in the Church, which was the opinion of the Pelagians.

3) The Confessionists say, and in this they agree with all Lutherans, that all the works of man, even of the justified, are mortal sins. The *Augsburg Confession*[14] indicates this, but Luther more clearly asserts it in his *Assertions*,[15] whereby it seems to follow that no man is in the Church. For, if only the just are in the Church, and there are altogether no just in the world, and naturally when the works of every man are sins, who, I ask, will

---

[14] Articl. 6 & 20.

[15] artc. 32.

8

constitute the Church? But they easily explain the whole matter when they say the works of the just are all mortal sins, but still they are not imputed to them if they have the faith, and hence he who has faith, at the same time is the most just and also sins by every work. In some manner the Confessionists agree with the Donatists and the Novationists. For, as they did not exclude all sinners from the Church, but only those who committed idolatry, so the former do not exclude all sinners, but only those who do not truly believe. For they think, as we said, that no crime is imputed to believers.

The fifth opinion seems to have been raked together from all these. For it teaches that the Church is constituted from the predestined. Thus Calvin taught three things in this regard. 1) Once someone has faith, he can never be damned, and furthermore all who have the faith are necessarily predestined. He holds this in the *Institutes*,[16] but the ancient heretic Jovinian expressly taught this same thing in the ancient Church, as we see from St. Jerome.[17] 2) He also teaches that the true Church can be recognized by God alone since its foundation is divine election, because it is constituted from the faithful, who are necessary from the number of the elect.[18] 3) he teaches besides a certain external Church, wherein the good and

---

[16] lib. 3, ca. 2, §8-11.

[17] *Contra Iovinianum*, lib. 2.

[18] *Instit.*, lib. 3, cap. 1, §2 and to a lesser degree in cap. 8, §4 et sequentibus.

the bad dwell, as the Confessionsts said above, he holds in the same book and chapter, in the subsequent sections. Martin Bucer seems to think the same thing and he defines the kingdom of Christ as the charge of salvation of the elect of God, whom God has gathered on earth.[19] Tilman Hesch teaches the same thing.[20]

The Catholic teaching is that the Church is only one, not two, and that the body of men of the same Christian profession and of the same Sacraments gathered in communion is one and true, under the rule of legitimate pastors and especially of the one Vicar of Christ on Earth, the Roman Pontiff. From such a definition it can be clearly understood which men pertain to the Church and which do not. For there are three parts of this definition; the profession of the true faith, the communion of the Sacraments, and subjection to the legitimate pastor, the Roman Pontiff. By the reasoning of the first all infidels and those who have never entered the Church are excluded, such as Jews, Turks, and Pagans; then those who were in the Church but left, such as heretics and apostates. By the reasoning of the second part, all Catechumens and excommunicates are excluded, because they have not been admitted to the communion of the Sacraments, these are sent out; by reasoning of the third, all schismatics are excluded, that is those who have the faith and the Sacraments, but are not under the legitimate

---

[19] *De regno Christi*, lib. 1, cap. 5.

[20] *De erroribus Pontificorum*, locus 12; *de Ecclesia*, lib. 1, cap. 3.

pastor, and therefore profess the faith and receive the Sacraments outside of the Church. Yet, all others, even the base, wicked and impious are included.

This is the difference between our teaching and all others, that all others require external virtues to constitute someone in the Church, and for that reason they make the Church invisible; but even though we believe all virtues (e.g. faith, hope and charity and the rest), are discovered in the Church, still that someone could absolutely be called part of the true Church, on which the Scriptures speak, we do not think any internal virtue is required, but only the external profession of faith, as well as the communion of the Sacraments which is taken up in that sense. For the Church is a body of men that is just as visible and palpable as the body of the Roman people, or the Kingdom of France, or the Republic of Venice.

Furthermore, it must be noted with Augustine,[21] that the Church is a living body in which there is a soul and body, and in the soul there are internal gifts of the Holy Spirit, namely Faith, Hope and Charity, etc. The body is the external profession of faith as well as the communication of the Sacraments. From there it happens that some men are in the soul and body of the Church and furthermore are united to Christ the head inwardly and outwardly, and such are perfectly in the Church, since they are as living members in the body, although among them are also some who participate more or less in the life

---

[21] *Breviculus collation.*, collat. 3.

of the Church, and some even who might hold only the beginning of life like a sense but not a motion, just as those who only have faith without charity. Again, some might be in the soul of the Church and not in the body, such as Catechumens or the excommunicated if they might have faith and charity, which can happen. Then, some may be in the body, but not the soul, such as those who have no internal virtue, and still by hope, or by some temporal fear profess the faith and communicate in the Sacraments under the rule of their pastors, and such are like hairs or nails, or bad humors in the human body.

Therefore, our definition holds true in this last manner of being in the Church, because this at least is required, that one can be said to be apart of the visible Church. Therefore, it must in the proper order be proved that the following do not pertain to the Church: the unbaptized, heretics, apostates, excommunicates and schismatics. Next, that those who are not predestined do in fact pertain to the Church, along with the imperfect and also manifest sinners; then lastly, secret heretics, if they would have the Sacraments as well as the profession of faith and subjection to the Church, etc.

# CHAPTER III
## *On the Unbaptized*

AUL certainly speaks about the unbaptized infidels when he says,[1] "Why do you ask me to judge concerning those who are outside?" He says generally in that passage that they are outside who did not give their names for Christ through Baptism, but followed some other religions.

On Catechumens, there is a somewhat greater difficulty because they are faithful, and can be saved if they die in that state but still no man can be saved outside the Church, just as no one could outside of the ark of Noah, according to that which is held in the first chapter of the Lateran Council (III): "The universal Church of the faithful is one, outside of which altogether no one is saved." But just the same, it is certain that Catechumens are not in the Church properly and by act, but only in potency, just as in the way a man being conceived but not yet formed and born is not called a man, except in potency. For we read in Acts II: "Therefore those who received the word were baptized and on that day around three thousand were added." Likewise, the Council of Florence in the instruction of the Armenians teaches that men become members of Christ and concern the body of

---

[1] 1 Cor. 5:12.

the Church when they are baptized, and the Fathers teach likewise.

St. Gregory Nazianzen, in his oration on holy Baptism, says that Catechumens are in the vestibule of piety, but still they cannot be called faithful unless they enter in through Baptism. John Chrysostom says that Catechumens are foreign to the faithful and have nothing in common with them, not citizenship, nor table, etc.[2] Tertullian in the *Praescriptiones*, condemns among the heretics those that refused to distinguish the Catechumens from the faithful. Cyril teaches that Catechumens are with Christians just as the uncircumcised were among the Jews, who on that account could not feed on the Paschal lamb.[3] Augustine distinguished Catechumens from the faithful, which other Fathers also do.[4] Moreover, it is certain that the Church is the body of the faithful.

Therefore, Catechumens do not have the right to any sacraments, nor to other things which are common to the universal Church. Therefore Catechumens do not pertain to the Church properly or in act. Therefore, how, you will ask, are they saved, if they are outside the Church? The author of the book on Ecclesiastical dogmas (cap. 74) clearly responds, that Catechumens are not saved. But this seems too harsh. Certainly St. Ambrose in his oration on the death of Valentinian affirms with clear words that

---

[2] hom. 24 in Ioannem.

[3] Lib. 12 in Ioan., cap. 50.

[4] Tract 4 in Ioannem and elsewhere,

Catechumens (in which Valentinian was numbered) can be saved when they have departed from this life.

Therefore, there is another solution. Melchior Cano says that Catechumens can be saved because even if they are not of the Church, which properly is called Christian, still they are part of the Church which embraces all the faithful from Abel even to the consummation of the world. But this does not seem to satisfy. For after the coming of Christ there is no true Church but that which is properly called Christian; consequently, if Catechumens are not in it, they are in nothing.

Consequently, I respond that it is said outside the Church no man is saved, and this ought to be understood on those who are neither in fact nor in desire within the Church, just as all the Theologians commonly teach on Baptism. Moreover, if the Catechumens are not in the Church *de facto*, at least they are in the Church in desire, therefore they can be saved. This is not opposed to the similitude of the Ark of Noah (outside of which no man was saved), even if he were in it by desire since similitudes do not agree in all things. For that reason, 1 Peter 3 compares Baptism to the ark of Noah and still it is certain that some are saved without Baptism in fact.

But, one might say, Augustine says that Catechumens are in the Church;[5] it is true, but in the same place he separates them from the faithful. Therefore, he meant that they are in the Church not by act, but by potency, which

---

[5] Tract. 4 in Ioannem.

he explains in the beginning of the 2nd book on the Creed, where he compares Catechumens to men who are conceived but not yet born.

## CHAPTER IV
*On Heretics and Apostates*

A LONSO DE CASTRO teaches that heretics and baptized apostates are members and parts of the Church, even if they openly profess a false doctrine.[1] Such an opinion is clearly false, and it can easily be refuted. 1) Scripture shows this, since in 1 Timothy 1:19 it says that certain men are shipwrecked in regard to the faith. In that passage, it understands heretics by means of a metaphor of a shipwreck, after being broken from one part of the boat of the Church, after which they sink into the sea, which also is meant by the Lord's parable of the net which is torn before the multitude.[2] Besides, to Titus he says, "after a heretic has been given one or two corrections, knowing that he is subversive, who is of this sort, he has been condemned by his own judgment." There the Apostle commands the Bishop that he should avoid heretics, because certainly he would not command it if they were within the Church. For a shepherd ought not avoid those whom he has care of when they pertain to his own flock. And he adds the reason that such a pertinacious heretic is condemned by his own judgment, that is (as Jerome explains it), he has not been thrown out

---

[1] *De Justa haereticorum punitione*, lib. 2, cap. 2.

[2] Luke 5.

of the Church by excommunication, as many other sinners, but he cast himself out of the Church. Likewise, 1 John II says, "They went out from us, but they were not from among us," in other words, they went out from us because they were with us in the same Church but they were not from us according to divine election, as St. Augustine explains.[3]

2) This is proved from the 18th and 19th chapter of the Council of Nicaea, where heretics are said to be able to be received in the Church if they wish to return to it, although under certain conditions. In like manner, from the chapter *Firmiter* of the Lateran Council, on the Supreme Trinity and the Catholic Faith, where the Church is called the congregation of the faithful. It is certain that heretics are not in any manner among the faithful.

3) From the Fathers, Irenaeus says that Polycarp converted many heretics to the Church,[4] whence it follows that beforehand they had gone out from the Church. Tertullian says that when Marcion wanted to rejoin the Church, he received the same condition as the others that he had perverted, that he should be restored to the Church.[5] Cyprian says, in an epistle to Jubaianum, that heretics, although they are outside the Church, still claim the power of the Church for themselves after the fashion

---

[3] *de bono persever.*, cap. 8.

[4] Lib. 3, cap. 3.

[5] *De Praescriptionibus.*

of apes who, although they are not men, nevertheless wish to appear as men.

Jerome says, in his Dialogue against the Luciferians, "If you will have heard anywhere some who are called "Christs", not by the Lord Jesus Christ, but by some other name, as the Marcionists, Valentinians, Montanists, or Campenses, know that this is not the Church of Christ, but it is the Synagogue of Antichrist."

St. Augustine says sometimes it may happen that a heretic who is outside the Church might not act against it, while a Catholic inside the Church might act against it.[6] And in his book on the Unity of the Church, chapter IV: "Those who do not believe that Christ came in the flesh from the Virgin Mary, from the seed of David or that he rose in his own body in which he was crucified and buried, indeed they are not in the Church."

Lastly, it happens that when the Church was a united multitude (for a certain people are either a kingdom, or one body) and this particular union consists in the profession of the one faith, the observance of the same laws and rights; no reason permits that we might say they are of the body of the Church who have altogether no union with it.

On the other hand, some object firstly with what is said in Matthew on the parable of the cockle the three that are discovered in the same field, wheat, the husks and the chaff, which mean good Catholics, bad Catholics and

---

[6] *Contra Donatistas*, lib. 4, cap. 10.

heretics, as Augustine[7] and Jerome explain on this passage, as well as Chrysostom. Moreover, the Church would be sick, as Cyprian[8] and Augustine[9] teach.

I respond: Some understand through cockle not heretics but wicked men who are in the Church. Thus Cyprian (loc. cit.) and often Augustine,[10] speaking not so much from his own opinion as much as by the mind of Cyprian. Moreover, the fact is Cyprian does not understand heretics by cockle, thereupon it can be understood that in those citations, where he says the cockle is in the Church, he says that heretics are not in the Church. Besides, the fact is made plain from the intention of Cyprian who writes in those places against the Novatianists, who refused to admit the lapsed penitents into the Church, fearing lest they might communicate their sins with others. Cyprian showed them that by the Lord's parable there are not only strong men in the Church but also weak who fall at some point, just as the cockle is in the field at the same time as the grain.

But although such an exposition might not be condemned and is not contrary to our position, nevertheless it seems better to respond with what Augustine says, that the field does not mean the Church,

---

[7] Quaest. 11 super Matthaeum.

[8] Lib. 3, epist. 3.

[9] Lib. 2, *Contra Cresconium*, cap. 34.

[10] Lib. 4, ep. 2.

but the whole world.[11] For the Lord, explaining the parable, says the field is the world. Hence, by the name of "cockle," although heretics are rightly understood, still perhaps we might understand it more literally as all the wicked in general, whether they be heretics or not. The scope of the parable, therefore, is to show that there were always going to be some wicked men in the world, nor can any human diligence cleanse the world before the day of judgment. For that reason, the Lord says that the cockle are the wicked sons, and all those who at length will be cast into eternal fire.

Secondly, they object with the verse in 2 Timothy 2:20, "In a great house there are vessels, some golden, some silver, some wooden, and some clay." There by the name *house* it seems that Paul understands the Church and by the name of the wooden and clay vessels, heretics. Thus he said a little earlier: "Their word creeps like a crab, from which are Hymnaeus and Philetus who are cut off from the truth."[12] Moreover, the house is understood as the Church which Cyprian,[13] Ambrose (in his commentary on this passage), and Augustine[14] teach.

I respond: This varies in the expositions of the Fathers. One is of the Greek Fathers, Chrysostom and Theophylactus who understand by the word house not the

---

[11] Quest. 11 super Matthaeum.

[12] 2 Tim. 2:17.

[13] Lib. 3, epist 3; lib. 4 epist. 2.

[14] Lib. 4 de Baptismo, cap. 12.

Church, but the world just as we said about the field in which there is cockle. The other is of the Latins, Cyprian, Ambrose and Augustine, who understand the house to be the Church. Although Augustine and Ambrose would have it that the wood and clay vessels represent heretics, nevertheless Augustine explains that same passage must be understood in the sense that they are in the Church, when he says they are in it before they are separated from it by obstinacy and pertinacity, and this is the time the Apostle considers, so that they are not heretics as much as they are said to be erring in the Church.[15] He also adds that it can be said they are in the Church after they have left it, on account of the administration of the Sacraments, because even they truly administer some sacraments. In other words, they are in the Church according to something, not on their own account. Ambrose receives it as the Church in a broad sense that is more common than proper, according to how it embraces all who are named Christians in any manner, in the same way that the Pagans usually said that in the body of Christians there are many opposed opinions and sects.

But according to Cyprian (whose explanation I reckon is more true), through wooden and clay vessels heretics are not understood, but the weak and frail who are easily seduced. When the Apostle says that in a great house there are vessels of gold, silver, etc., he is not referring to "whose word lurks like a crab", whereby Hymnaeus and

---

[15] *De Baptismo*, lib. 3, cap. 19.

Philetus are cut off from the truth, but to the part where he says: "And they overturn the faith of some men." The Apostle means that if they overturn some, they are not a danger for this reason, lest all would be overturned. For in the Church there are the strong and the weak, etc.

But one might say that Augustine, who understands heretics by the wooden and clay vessels, says he is moved to think this by Cyprian's words in his epistle to Antioninus, which is the second of book 4.

I respond: Augustine thought these words of the Apostle were related by Cyprian: "In a great house there are golden vessels, etc.," referred to the verse "whose word creeps like a crab," just as he says. Moreover, the words of Cyprian do not sound that way, and Cyprian correctly did not mean that heretics are in the Church, as is clear from the same epistle, where he clearly says that Novation is outside of the Church because he is a heretic.

Thirdly, the argument is made that the Church can judge and punish heretics, therefore they are within it, "For what is it to me to judge those who are on the outside?"[16] Besides, heretics retain the character of Baptism and priesthood, therefore they are Christians and priests.

I respond: Although heretics are not in the Church, nevertheless they ought to be; hence they pertain to her like sheep to the sheepfold when they roam outside the sheepfold. The Church can judge concerning those who

---

[16] 1 Cor. 5:12.

23

are inside by that very fact, or who ought to be, just as a pastor really can judge and compel the sheep who wander outside of the sheepfold through the mountains to return to it. In the same way, a general can compel by force a deserter from the army who has fled across to the camp of the enemy to return or even to hang him. The Apostle, on the other hand, speaks on those who were never truly in the Church.

Now I speak to that which relates to the character. Heretics retain those indelible characters outside of the Church, just as lost sheep retain the branding in their back and deserters of the army military signs: but they are not in the Church for that reason because those characters do not suffice to constitute someone in the Church; otherwise the Church would also be in hell. St. Thomas Aquinas says that the damned are not members of Christ in either act or potency.[17] Besides, the character does not properly unite a man with the head, rather it is a sign of the power of a certain union, and consequently, in hell they are recognized by that sign as men who were members of Christ. Nevertheless, that it does not unite them is clear since something that is invisible cannot unite outwardly, nor interiorly when it is not in act or when it is not an operative habit. For that reason St. Thomas places the first internal union in faith.

---

[17] III, Q. 8, art. 3.

## CHAPTER V
### *On Schismatics*

SEVERAL Catholics deliberate whether schismatics are in the Church, on the other hand there are those who affirm that they are in the Church, such as Alonso de Castro in the place we cited. Yet it is easy to teach the contrary from the Scripture and from the tradition of the Fathers. In the first place, when it is said in Luke that the nets were torn,[1] schisms in the Church are understood through the tearing of the nets and the exit of the fish from it, and the exit of heretics and schismatics, as St. Augustine explains.[2]

Besides, Scripture calls the Church, "One sheepfold,"[3] "One body,"[4] "One spouse, friend and dove."[5] Moreover, schism tears that which was one into parts, as is clear from its very name, as ó÷œæåéí [schizein] is to tear, and ó÷éóiÞ [schismç] means a tear. Consequently, schismatics are not in the Church nor are they of the Church. For the part that is torn from the body is no longer a part of that

---

[1] Luke 5:6.

[2] Tract. 122 *in Ioannem.*

[3] John 10:16.

[4] Rom. 12:5.

[5] Cant. 6:8.

body. For that reason Cyprian beautifully says that the Church is signified through the seamless garment of Christ which was not torn, that we might understand the Church can be torn, but not in that manner in which a garment is torn, so that some parts remain equally part of the garment, but how a branch is torn from a tree, which dies right away while the tree still lives.[6] In like manner, he adds it is similar to a river from its source which soon dries up while the source flows, and the ray from the sun, which fails right away while the sun remains as it was. Or, if one were to contend that the part torn from the Church is also a certain Church, then he would make many Churches; but that is against the Scriptures recently cited.

Secondly it is proved from the decrees of Pope Pelagius, who clearly proves that schismatics are not part of the Church.[7] Moreover, the testimony of the whole Church witnesses the fact, since on Good Friday it prays for heretics and schismatics that God would deign to recall them to the Catholic Church, which would not be the case if it believed they were in the Church. The testimony of the Roman Catechism also pertains to this, which is of no scanty authority in the Church of God. Thus the Catechism separates schismatics from the Church in its explanation of the Creed.[8]

---

[6] *De Unitate Ecclesiae.*

[7] 24.q.1, can. *Pudenda*, et can. *Schisma.*

[8] *Catechism of the Council of Trent*, Part I: The Creed, Article IX.

Thirdly, it is proved from the Fathers. Irenaeus, after he had said earlier in his work that a spiritual man judges all heretics and schismatics and had enumerated them into many particular heresies, he also had added them under those properly called schismatic, and he concludes in the end: "He will judge all those who are outside the truth, that is outside the Church."[9] St. Cyprian says, "The people has been joined to the priest even as the flock adheres to its shepherd, for that reason you ought to know that the Bishop is in the Church and the Church in the Bishop, and if there would be someone who is not with the bishop, he is not in the Church."[10] But certainly schismatics are not with the Bishop; therefore they are not in the Church.

Chrysostom said, "The meaning of schism convicts them enough, or rather more its name is enough to strike them, since they had not become many parts, rather the one had perished. For they constituted these many into whole Churches."[11] And in another homily he teaches that schismatics are like a hand that is cut from the body which soon ceases to be a member and he says in the same place that schismatics are in another Church even if they agree with the true Church of Christ in faith and doctrines.[12]

---

[9] Lib. 4, cap. 62.

[10] Lib. 4, epist. 9 ad Florentium Papianum.

[11] Hom. 3 in 1 Cor.

[12] Hom. 11 in epistolam ad Ephesios.

Jerome says, "Schismatics really separate a deceived multitude from the Church of God; still they do not do this from belief, as heretics do."[13] And again, "We hold this is between heresy and schism, because a heresy holds a perverse doctrine, but schism equally separates from the Church by reason of Episcopal dissension."[14] There note the word *equally.*

Augustine says: "We believe in the Holy *Catholic* Church, since even the heretics and schismatics call their congregations "Churches", but the heretics violate faith in God by believing false things, while the schismatics leap from fraternal charity by wicked dissensions, even if they believe what we believe. For that very reason neither the heretic pertains to the Catholic Church because he loves God nor the schismatic because he loves his neighbor."[15]

Optatus of Miletus, speaking of schismatics, says: "After deserting their Catholic mother, the wicked sons run about outside of her and separate themselves, as you have done, being cut off from the root of the hated mother Church by sickles, like rebels who recede by wandering away."[16] In book 2 of that work he compares schismatics with branches, rivers and rays cut off from the tree, font and sun. Fulgentius says: "Hold most firmly and do not by any means doubt that not only Pagans but also Jews,

---

[13] In Caput Primum Amos.

[14] in cap. 3 ad Titum.

[15] *De Fide et Symbolo,* cap. 10.

[16] *Contra Parmenianum,* lib. 1.

heretics and schismatics who end the present life outside the Catholic Church are going into the eternal fire."[17] Next Thomas Waldens holds the same thing,[18] as well as John Driedo,[19] and other more recent writers.

Lastly, it is proven from reason. From the very notion of what the Church is, that it is one in regard to the union of members within her, and with her head, but schism abolishes this union since it separates itself from communion with the head and other members. Moreover the essential unity of the Church consists in that union of that joining of the members among and with the head is proven, since there is a manifold unity discovered in the Church. 1) The unity of the same beginning; that is the calling of God. "No one comes to me, etc."[20] 2) The unity by reason of the same final end, which is signified in Matthew 20 in that one denarius promised to all the workers. 3) By reason of the same means, that is the Faith, Sacraments, and laws according to what is said in Ephesians 4, "One faith, one baptism." 4) By unity of the same Holy Spirit, by whom the Universal Church is steered as if by an external and separate Captain, "There are divisions of grace, but the same Spirit."[21] 5) By reason

---

[17] *De fide ad Petrum*, cap. 38 et 39.

[18] 1 lib. 2, cap. 9 doctrinalis fidei antiquae.

[19] Lib. 4 de Scripturis et dogmatibus Ecclesiasticis, cap. 2, part. 2.

[20] John 6.

[21] 1 Cor. 12:4.

of the same head, just as an internal and continuous Captain; for every Church obeys the same Christ and his vicar just like a head, "He gave the him as the head over the whole Church,"[22] and, "Simon Peter, feed my sheep."[23] 6) By reason of the connection of the members among themselves and especially with the head as the principal member, "We are one body, each one members of another."[24]

Moreover, among these unities we have enumerated that properly make one Church there are two ends. By the first, the Church is not one as much as it is from one. By the second, it is not as much one as to one. By the third it is not as much one as through one. By the fourth it is not as much one as under one. By the fifth and sixth, it is properly one, that is one body, one people and one society. Schism, however, is opposed to these last unities; consequently there is schism when one member refuses to be any longer a member of that body, nor under the head, this is the reason why it abolishes the essential unity and also the Church herself; therefore a schismatic is not of the Church.

Now they object: 1) The Church is a congregation of Catholics, as Pope Nicholas defined (*De Consecrat.*, distinctione prima, can. Ecclesia), But schismatics are Catholics, therefore they are of the Church.

---

[22] Ephesians 1:22.

[23] John 21.

[24] Romans 12:5.

I respond: Firstly, even if schismatics have the Catholic faith, nevertheless, they cannot properly be called Catholics even if they profess the faith in the Catholic Church, as is clear from the citations we provided from St. Augustine and Optatus. I say secondly, this is not the full definition of Pope Nicholas, nor did he mean to define the Church but only exclude heretics from the Church. Just as Innocent did when he said that the Church is the congregation of the faithful.[25]

They object 2) Even if schismatics refuse to submit to the Pope, nevertheless they mean to submit to Christ the Supreme Head, and although they refuse to communicate with this Church on earth, nevertheless, they mean to communicate with the Church that is in heaven, namely the better part of the Church, therefore they do not abolish the unity of the Church nor are they absolutely outside it. This argument is confirmed from like things. For if anyone would refuse to be under his particular Bishop nor communicate with that particular Church under that Bishop, and nevertheless he means to be under the Roman Pontiff and communicates with the universal Church, he cannot be said to be outside the Church.

I respond: No man can be under Christ and communicate with the Church who is not subject to the Pope and is not in communion with the Church militant—even if he wishes to be. For Christ said, "He who hears you, hears me," (Luke 10:16) and besides, just as

---

[25] cap. *Firmiter, de Summa Trinitate et fide Catholica.*

Christ is the supreme head in regard to the interior life (since he breaths sense and motion into his members, that is faith and charity), so the Pope is the supreme head over the Church militant, in regard to the exterior life of the doctrine and the sacraments. Furthermore, the Church triumphant is united, nay more, it is one with the Church militant, and hence no man can be separated from one without being separated from the other.

In a similar fashion I respond with a confirmation. One who separates himself from a particular Church and Bishop is necessarily separated from the Church and the universal Bishop (unless perhaps someone had done it because that particular Church and its bishop were heretics or schismatics). For Cyprian rightly says, "They deceive themselves in vain, who, not having peace with the priests of God, creep and believe that they secretly communicate with the Church, which is Catholic and one and that it would not be torn nor divided but really is the connection of those adhering to each other and joined with the glue of the priests.[26]

---

[26] Lib. 4, ep. 9.

## CHAPTER VI
### *On the Excommunicated*

ONCERNING the Excommunicated, the Roman Catechism teaches they are not in the Church.[1] Furthermore, Thomas Waldens,[2] Juan Torquemada,[3] John Driedo[4] and several others teach the same thing. It is proven first from what we read in Matthew 18:17, "If they will not listen to the Church, let him be to you as a heathen and a tax-collector." There the Lord speaks about the excommunicated according to the exposition of all. Heathens are not in the Church. Likewise we see in 1 Corinthinas, "Have you not rather not mourned that he is taken away from your midst, that did such a thing? . . . Do you not know that a little leaven corrupts the whole mass? . . . Put away the evil one from yourselves."[5] With these words, the Apostle describes what it means to be excommunicated. For he bids anyone to be excommunicated who would have the wife of his father.

---

[1] Part I, *In explication of the Creed*, Article IX.

[2] *Doctr. fid. antiquae*, tom. 1, lib. 2, cap. 9.

[3] *Summae de Ecclesia*, lib. 1, cap. 3.

[4] *De Script. et dogmatibus Ecclesiasticis*, lib. 4, cap. 2, part. 2

[5] 1 Cor. 5:2, 6, 13.

Secondly it is proved from Canon law, "It is canonically established, following the examples of the holy Fathers, that we eliminate violators of the Church of God from the lap of holy mother the Church and the consort with the whole Christian world by the authority of God and the judgment of the Holy Spirit."[6]

Thirdly from the Fathers. Eusebius, relating the extent to which Pope Victor had excommunicated all the Galatians says, "He sent a letter in which he separated everyone at the same time without distinction from Ecclesiastical union.... Irenaeus argued with Victor because it was not right to cut so many and such Churches from the unity of the body."[7] Epiphanius, speaking about Marcion (who had professed virginity prior to becoming a heretic and nevertheless violated a woman who also had professed virginity and consequently was excommunicated by his father), said, "He was ejected from the Church by his own father, for his father was famous due to the excellence of his piety and persevered living honestly in the ministry of the episcopate."[8]

Hilary, commenting on that verse, "Let him be to you as a heathen and a tax-collector," says that God did that very thing with the people of Israel as Christ advises must be done. Firstly, he corrected the people between him and

---

[6] 11, q. 3, can. *Canonica.*

[7] *Historiae,* lib. 5, cap. 24.

[8] Haeres. 42, which is of Marcion.

it alone, when he appeared to them with majesty on mount Sinai. Secondly, he applied two witnesses to himself, that is the Law and the Prophets. Third, he spoke to the Church, that is, he sent Christ as the Supreme Prelate of the Church who reproached the Jews. Lastly, when they did not listen to the prelate of the Church, he neglected them and left them behind, just as the heathen and the tax-collectors. With such words he showed that through excommunication a man becomes just as a heathen and a tax-collector, cast out from the people of God, and no longer governed by that peculiar providence whereby the Church is governed.

Chrysostom and Theophylactus explain on this citation that one is said to be cast out from the Church because he becomes as a heathen and a tax-collector. Jerome says that some sinners are pushed outside the Church through the excommunications of bishops and become heretics and schismatics by their very own will. Augustine says that those who are excommunicated are visibly cut from the body of the Church.[9] Likewise he says that through excommunication diseased sheep are separated from the healthy lest dangerous plagues creep through a great many of them.[10] This opinion is cited by Augustine: "Every Christian who is excommunicated by priests is handed over to Satan. How? Because obviously the devil is outside the Church, just as Christ is in the

---

[9] Lib. *de unitate Ecclesiae,* last chapter.

[10] *De Corrept. et Gratia,* cap. 15.

Church."[11] Anselm subscribes to this when says that a man is handed over to Satan that is pushed out of the Church through excommunication.[12]

Lastly it is proven by reason. Firstly, by excommunication men are deprived from all the spiritual privileges that men in the Church have, as Tertullian teaches;[13] consequently they are no longer in the body of the Church. What is it for some citizen to be deprived of his city except to be deprived of all privileges that are due to men of that city? Secondly, excommunication has that place in the Church that the death penalty had in the Old Testament as well as in the temporal commonwealth. Yet, through death men are clearly separated from the whole commonwealth. Augustine says, "Excommunication now does in the Church what death did formerly."[14] There he compares what is said in Deuteronomy 24:7, "You will abolish the evil one from your midst," with what Paul says, "Remove the wicked man from your presence."[15] Thirdly, there is no penalty that the Church can inflict that is more severe than excommunication, as St. Augustine teaches,[16] therefore by excommunication a man is cast out from the Church. It is more serious to be cast

---

[11] 11, quaest. 11, 3 can. Omnis.

[12] In 1 Cor. V.

[13] *Apologeticus*, cap. 39.

[14] Quaest. 39 in Deuteron.

[15] 1 Cor. V:13.

[16] *De Correptione et Gratia*, cap. 15.

from the Church than any penalty you like that remains for the Church to take up.

Fourthly, excommunication can not be imposed except upon those who are contumacious and incorrigible, as St. Augustine teaches.[17] And indeed, even all Theologians deduce this from that passage of Matthew 18:17 which we have been citing. Consequently, excommunication is the ejection from the Church; for if excommunication were to be imposed for some penalty short of ejection, it would also be imposed in every degree whatsoever upon murderers, adulterers and other malefactors even if they are not contumacious. Add to this that when the excommunicates are absolved, it is said: "Now you have been restored to the unity of the Church and the participation of the members." That is a clear sign that the excommunicates were separated from the unity of the Church.

But some object to the contrary. First, an excommunicated man remains baptized, retains the profession of faith and the subjection of the legitimate prelate, and to the extent that he is a friend of God, if he will be unjustly excommunicated then the excommunicate can also justly do penance and have those three before he is absolved, therefore he will be in the Church, even while remaining excommunicated.

*I respond:* Such a person is in the Church by his mind, or by desire, which suffices to salvation, but still not in the

---

[17] *De Vera Religione*, cap. 6.

body or the external communion which properly causes a man to be in this visible Church which is on Earth. Augustine says, "Often divine providence may permit that even good men may be expelled from the Christian congregation. If men will bear such contumely or injury very patiently for the peace of the Church, nor will have created any novelties, schisms or heresies then they will teach men how truly God must be served by good will and by such genuine charity. The Father who sees in secret will crown men of this sort in secret."[18]

Secondly, our adversaries raise objections because Augustine says, "And we do not separate from the people of God those whom we reduce to a lower place by degradation or excommunication."[19]

I respond: I suspect this passage has been corrupted and thus the phrase "And we do not separate from the people of God," must be picked out, since what follows after that is, "And we are not allowed to do this for the sake of peace and tranquility of the Church, still we do not so neglect the Church, but we tolerate that which we refuse to arrive where we wish, using the precaution of the Lord's precept, lest we might wish to gather the cockle before its time and eradicate the wheat with it." But if this passage has not been corrupted then the response can be made that through the words, "the people of God," not only the Church militant is understood but the absolute

---

[18] *De Vera Religione*, cap. 6.

[19] *Contra Donatistas*, cap. 20.

number of those going to be saved, whether they might be in the Church or whether they can be; since by excommunication pastors do not intend to separate men from the number of those who can be saved, but rather more to help them to salvation by that correction.

Our adversaries object thirdly that excommunication is a type of spiritual medicine established for the assistance of those who are excommunicated. For this reason the Apostle says, "But if any man does not obey our word by epistle, mark such a man lest you keep company with him so that he shall be ashamed."[20]

I respond: Excommunication, even if it tears a man from the Church, nevertheless does not take away potency so that he cannot again be inserted into the Church when he is cut off from it if he should do penance. Therefore, the Church, through excommunication, separates certain men from its body, but for their sake because she desires them to be humbled by that shame, and once humbled then received again into the body of the Church.

---

[20] 2 Thess. 3:14.

OREOVER, the fact that not only the predestined but even the reprobate can pertain to the Church (contrary to Wycliffe and Calvin) must be proved. 1) From the very clear parables of the Lord. In Matthew the Church is compared with a threshing floor, "He will clear his threshing floor and will gather the wheat into his barn, but he will burn the chaff in the inextinguishable fire."[1] Certainly the term "threshing floor" cannot be understood except about the Church, in which the threshing floor is discovered, but the part about the inextinguishable fire cannot be understood about the elect. Later in Matthew he compares the net let down in the sea that gathers every kind of fish but at length some of them are sent into the furnace of fire,[2] but that certainly is not said about the predestined.

Later in Matthew's Gospel the nuptial dinner is compared to that in which the good and the wicked enter and afterward the wicked do not have the nuptial garment and are cast into exterior darkness. Then the Lord concludes it saying, "Many are called but few are chosen,"[3] *i.e.*, many are in the Church, which is a certain evocation,

---

[1] Matthew 3:12.

[2] Matthew 13:47-50.

[3] Matthew 22:14.

or the body of those called who still are of the elect. Likewise he compares it to ten virgins, of whom the five prudent will enter the nuptials with the spouse on the day of judgment, but the five foolish will be excluded.[4] In the same place it is compared to a sheepfold in which there are sheep and goats and the former, as the Lord himself explains, are the elect while the latter are the reprobate.[5] Paul bids the incestuous to be expelled from the Church,[6] and still he could not cause him to be cast out from the predestined, nor did he will it, since he cast him out that, having been humbled, he would return and be saved on the day of the Lord, as he says in the same place.[7] Likewise in 2 Timothy 2:20 he says, "In a great house there are vessels, some gold and silver, some wooden and made of clay, some in glory and some in contumely." There does not seem to be a doubt that the vessels in glory are the elect while the vessels in contumely are the reprobate even though they are in the same house.

St. Cyprian confirms the same thing[8] and he clearly teaches that in the Church there are wheat and cockle, as well as golden and wooden vessels, since it is certain that the cockle is burned and the wooden vessels are in contumely. Moreover St. Augustine says, "According to foreknowledge and predestination how many sheep are

---

[4] Matthew 25:1-12.

[5] Matthew 25:33.

[6] 1 Cor. 5:1-3.

[7] 1 Cor. 5:5.

[8] Lib. 3, epist. 3; lib. 4, epist. 2.

outside and how many wolves inside?"[9] There he says that many predestined are outside the Church and many reprobates are within it.

Besides, the examples of Paul and Judas agree with it. Jan Hus said that Paul was always in the Church but Judas was never in it. On the other hand, Paul himself says that he had persecuted the Church of God, just as Luke affirms.[10] Therefore I ask, was the Church which Paul persecuted the true Church, or it was not? If the true Church, then Paul was not a member of the true Church at some point. For how was he of the Church which he opposed with all his strength? If that was not the true Church, then Paul and Luke lie when they unreservedly call it the Church of God.

Hence, St. Augustine teaches that Paul, although he was predestined, was a wolf before the fact and a sheep afterward.[11] Chrysostom says that Paul was a clay vessel but turned into gold while Judas was gold but turned into clay.[12] Hence Judas became reprobate, as is clear from the Acts of the Apostles,[13] and nevertheless, was at some point in the true Church. It is said in the same passage of Acts that he was an Apostle from the twelve and was called a

---

[9] Tract. 45 in Ioannem. He repeats the same thing in *Contra Cresconium*, lib. 2, cap. 34.

[10] 1 Timothy 1:13; Galat. 1:13; Cor. 15:9; Acts 9:1.

[11] Serm 1, de conversione Sancti Pauli.

[12] Hom. 6 in II Tim.

[13] Acts 1.

Bishop by David,[14] This could not be true unless he were in the Church at some point. For this reason Augustine says that Judas was a son of Christ and still persecuted his father just as Absalom did David.[15] He also says that Judas was in the Church in which the rest of the Apostles were.[16]

Reason also agrees for if predestination alone makes a man in the Church, it would follow that if the Turks, Jews, heretics or any impious men were predestined, then they are now in the Church and the living members of Christ; but on the other hand certain holy and pious baptized men, if they might not be predestined, are not in the Church or the body of Christ. But each is false and against what is expressed in the Scripture. For above we showed the fact that the unbaptized and heretics are not in the Church, and the impious are not living members as it says in Romans, "If anyone does not have the spirit of Christ, he is not of him,"[17] *i.e.* a living member. That the impious do not have the spirit of Christ, but the spirit of the devil is clear from their works. For they are not patient, chaste, etc., which are works of the spirit, rather they are adulterers, murderers, blasphemers, etc., which are works of the flesh.[18] On the contrary, we find that all pious baptized men are members of the Church in Paul, "We are

---

[14] Psalm 108 (109).

[15] in Psalm 3.

[16] *De Unitate Ecclesiae*, cap. 13.

[17] Romans 8:9.

[18] Gal. 6:8.

all baptized in one spirit into one body,"[19] and again, "You are all sons of God through faith in Christ Jesus, whoever you are that have been baptized in Christ, have put on Christ."[20] And still it is not believable that all the Corinthians and Galatians were predestined.

Next, Augustine says, "In the bond of Christ, just as in a living building of the temple of God, which is the Church, men are born not from the works of justice that they do rather they are transferred by works of grace just as from the mass of a ruin to the solidity of a building."[21] Again, showing that the impious do not pertain to the living members of Christ, he says, "God forbid that they could enter the confines of the enclosed garden that has such a guard as cannot be deceived, who nevertheless if they confess and are corrected, then enter, then are cleansed, then are enclosed among the trees of the garden, then are numbered in the members of the singular dove."[22]

Lastly it is proven from what is disagreeable; for if only the predestined were in the Church, then everything would be uncertain. Then no man could recognize his brothers, nor would shepherds know their sheep or be recognized by them, since nobody would know who is predestined. Besides nobody would know which would be the true Scripture, which would be the true Sacraments, or

---

[19] 1 Cor. 12:13.

[20] Gal. 3:27.

[21] Epist. ad Dardanum.

[22] *Contra Cresconium*, lib. 2, cap. 21.

the true faith, etc., since all these depend upon the testimony of the true Church.

Yet they object to this with several arguments. 1) That verse in the Canticles, "An enclosed garden, a sealed font, a well of living water, etc.," without a doubt means the Church, and still St. Augustine explains all of these about the elect alone.[23]

I respond: Firstly, Scripture often attributes one thing by a figure of speech to the whole which only agrees with a part. In Matthew it says that the thieves that were crucified with the Lord blasphemed against him,[24] when it is certain from Luke that only one of them blasphemed.[25] In Philippians it says "All seek what is their own,"[26] and yet there were not very many saints like this who lived then and especially the Philippians. Secondly I say that what is said about the spouse in the Canticles must not necessarily be understood on the Church. Some men understand this to be about the Church, and others about the Blessed Virgin, and others every perfect soul (which seems more probable), for it is said, "There are sixty queens and eighty concubines and the young women are beyond number. One is my dove, my perfect, my mother is one chosen by her mother."[27] In that passage, if you understand the Church through that one spouse, what will

---

[23] *De Baptismo*, lib. 5, cap. 27.

[24] Matt. 27:39.

[25] Luke 23:40.

[26] Philippians 2:21.

[27] Canticle of Canticles 6:8.

you understand by the queens, concubines and young women? Therefore the Church is understood by the mother while the souls of the more imperfect by the queens, concubines and young women and at length the faithful and good souls. For it is said, "For that reason the young women have loved you."[28] But through the one perfect spouse and dove is understood a perfect soul. Thus it is also said in that very place, "Just as a lily among thorns, so my beloved among the daughters."[29] If you understand the Church through the beloved, what will you understand for the other daughters? Would it be the congregation of the unfaithful? God forbid. Thus, it speaks on the perfect soul, which is called to mind amidst the multitude of sinners in the same garden of the Church. St. Augustine says, "The thorns are described on account of the malignity of morals, the daughters are described on account of the communion of the Sacraments."[30]

2) They make the second objection that the ark of Noah was a figure of the Church, as Augustine teaches,[31] but there was nobody in the ark but those who were going to be saved from the waters, therefore only the predestined are in the Church.

I respond: Similitudes do not agree in all things, otherwise every baptized person would be predestined,

---

[28] cap.1.

[29] cap.2.

[30] Epist. 48.

[31] *de Baptismo*, lib. 5, cap. ult.

since Peter compares Baptism to the ark of Noah,[32] thus not only the good but even the wicked would be saved because in the ark both the clean and unclean animals were saved. For that very reason the ark agrees with the Church; for just as outside the ark no man could be saved, so not outside the Church, as Augustine remarks on that citation, as well as Cyprian and Jerome,[33] nor must any other similitude be sought out.

3) They make their third objection that Christ is not the head except of his Church which he will save, and which he will show to himself on the glorious day of judgment, not having spot or stain, as Paul says.[34] But only the predestined will be saved and glorious, consequently, only the predestined pertain to the Church of Christ.

I respond: When it is said that Christ is not the head except of his Church which he will save, that, "of his Church," can mean of his part of the Church which he will save, and then the proposition is false. For he is the head of his whole body although certain members are going to cease to be members and will perish in eternity. It can also mean, "of his Church," as in the whole Church, as is distinguished from other congregations of infidels and then the proposition is true but the consequent is bad. Although some members of this Church will not be saved,

---

[32] 1 Peter 3:20.

[33] Cyprian, *De unitate Ecclesiae.*; Jerome, epist. ad Damasum, de tribus Hypostatibus.

[34] Ephes. 5:27.

it does not follow on that account that Christ did not save his Church, of which he is the head.

4) They argue fourthly that the mystical body is like a true body, but the whole true body of Christ is safe and glorious with all its parts, therefore the mystical body in all of its members and parts ought to be saved.

I respond: Firstly, similitudes do not agree in all things. Secondly, just as the body of Christ is true, saved and glorious in regard to all its formal parts, still not in regard to all its material parts, for the material parts flowed out from and were changed in Christ as we see happens among us, so also the mystical body is going to be saved in regard to all the formal parts, which are Apostles, Prophets, Pastors, Teachers, etc.; some will be saved from every race of men, but not in regard to all material parts, which are all men individually.

5) The Church is one sheepfold,[35] but there are no sheep except the predestined,[36] therefore, only the predestined are in the Church.

I respond: In some places of Scripture the word "sheep" means only the predestined as in Matthew 25:33 where the sheep are separated from the goats, and in John 10:3, "My sheep hear my voice." In other places it means everyone in general, both the good and the bad who are in the Church, as in the last chapter of John, "Feed my sheep," and in the Psalms, "Your furor has been aroused over thy pasture,"[37]

---

[35] John 10:16.

[36] Augustine, Tractatu in *Ioannem* 45.

[37] Psal. 73 [74]:1.

and in Ezechiel 34:4, the sheep of God are described as some fat, some lean, some healthy and some sick, but according to this second meaning the argument does not have any force.

Still, we respond following the earlier meaning that in the sheepfold there are not only sheep but also goats, as is clear from Matthew 25:33, where they are separated since beforehand they were present together in the same sheepfold. Moreover, the sheepfold may still be so called even if it does not, for the most part contain only sheep. Just the same, Rome is called a city although she embraces many who are not her citizens.

6) They argue from John, "I have other sheep who are not from this sheepfold,"[38] and also, "Jesus was going to die for the nation, but not only for the nation but even that the sons of God who were dispersed would be gathered into one."[39] In such passages the predestined are called sheep and sons of God, even when they lived amidst the errors of the Gentiles, for this reason the predestined are always in the Church. Likewise we see in 2 Timothy, "The strong foundation of God stands having this seal, the Lord knew who were his own,"[40] and in 1 John, "They went out from us but they were not from us, for if they were from us they would certainly have remained with us."[41] Therefore, even before they went out they were not

---

[38] John 10:16.

[39] John 11:52.

[40] 2 Timothy 2:19.

[41] 1 John 2:19.

from us but seemed to be. And it is confirmed by
Augustine, "Some are sons of God because they received
grace temporally, as when it says 'from us,' nevertheless
they are not of God.... They went out from us, but they
were not of us, *i.e.* even when they seemed to be among us
they were not. Likewise, they were not sons even when
they seemed to be in profession and in the name of sons.
... because they did not have perseverance, just as they
were not truly disciples of Christ so they were not truly
sons of God, even when they seemed to be and were so
called."[42] Besides, in *Doctrina Christiana*, arguing with
Ticonius who called the mystical body of the Lord, *i.e.* the
Church, divided, he also says, "It ought not be so called,
for that part which will not be with him forever is not
really the Lord's body."[43]

I respond: Two distinct things must be noted for the
explanation of these passages. The first is that a man can
be called a sheep, a son, and a member of Christ in two
ways: a) according to predestination; b) according to
present justice. This distinction is contained with Paul, for
when he says, "Whoever does not have the spirit of Christ
is not of him,"[44] and nevertheless in 2 Timothy he says
about the predestined, "The Lord knows who are his
own."[45] Therefore, a member and a non-member of Christ
can be one and the same. For he will be his if he has been

---

[42] *De Corrept. et Gratia*, cap. 9.

[43] *loc. cit.*, lib. 3, ca. 32.

[44] Romans 8:9.

[45] 2 Timoth. 2:19.

predestined, and he will not be his if meanwhile he does not have his spirit. Likewise Augustine teaches, "According to foreknowledge, many who are certainly outside, and even those who are called heretics, are better than many and good Catholics." And again, "According to foreknowledge and predestination how many sheep are outside? But how many wolves are inside?"[46]

The difference between these is that those who are the sheep, sons, or members, are only so according to predestination, such as are by potency but not by act. For predestination places nothing in man, rather it is an act remaining in God himself. But those who are such according to present justice are simply such by act, because they really have this act in themselves, whence they are called such. Augustine clearly teaches this when he says, "Why is it that I said how many sheep are outside? How many that revel are going to be chaste? How many that blaspheme Christ are going to believe in Christ? And these are sheep. Even so, they only hear a foreign voice, they follow strangers. Likewise how many praise God on the inside but are going to blaspheme? How many are chaste but will fornicate and who now stand but are going to fall? And we say they are not sheep from the predestined."[47] There you can see how he speaks about the future, "they who revel are going to be chaste, etc." For in the same way it can be said that those who are outside are

---

[46] Tract. 45 in Ioan.; he says similar things in *de bono persever.*, cap. 8; *de corrept. et gratia*, cap. 9.

[47] Tract. 45 in Ioan.

52

going to be inside, and from this distinction it should be clear enough from the Scriptures we have brought forth. For there the sheep are spoken of, as well as the sons of God who still were not in the Church because they were such according to predestination and in potency, not however in act and simply.

For equal reasoning, it is said in 2 Timothy 2:19, "The Lord knows who are his," this phrase is about those who are his through predestination but not on the whole Church, since he adds in verse 20, "In a great house there are many vessels, some of gold, some silver, some wooden and others of clay." And the reprobate are similarly called those who went out from the Church and were not from us, because they were not from us according to predestination, although they were according to the communion of the Sacraments. In this way it ought also be understood what the author of the incomplete work says in homily 20 on Matthew, namely, that one who falls from the Church was never Christian; there he understands it according to predestination.

The second distinction is that one can truly be said to be a son of God or a member of the body of Christ in two ways, in one way by the truth of essence, or the form, and in the other way by the truth of the end, or as others say, from the truth of permanence. By the truth of essence it is the son of God who has charity. "Everyone who loves is born of God."[48] And likewise by the truth of essence is the member of Christ who lives in the same spirit. "In one

---

[48] 1 John 4:7.

spirit you all were baptized into one body."[49] But by the truth of the end one is called a son of God, who attains inheritance; and who will not attain it seemed to be a son but was not. For the purpose of descent is inheritance, "Such if a son and heir through God."[50] thus even by the truth of the end one is a member who will be saved, for Christ united the Church to himself for this purpose, just as the body to the head that he would save her, as it is said in Ephesians 4:16. Therefore, who is in grace and still has not been predestined, is truly a son and member by the truth of essence and is not truly a son or a member by the truth of the end. On the other hand, one who is not in grace, and still has been predestined, is not truly a son or a member by the truth of essence, and nevertheless is truly both by the truth of the end. The verse, "Who keeps his word, truly the charity of God has been perfected in him,"[51] is understood on the first truth; while the verse, "If you will have remained in my word, you will truly be my disciple,"[52] is on the second.

Since we have noted these things, the passages of Augustine will be easily understood, where he says that the just who are not predestined are neither truly sons nor members. For he speaks on the truth of the end, not on the truth of the essence, as he explains himself in the same passage. Likewise in his book on *Rebuke and Grace*, after

---

[49] 1 Cor. 12:13.

[50] Galat. 4:7.

[51] 1 John 2:5.

[52] John 8:31.

he had said the predestined—not the good—were truly sons,[53] he added, "Not because they feigned justice but because they did not remain in it." and in *Doctrina Christiana*,[54] rendering an account as to why he had said that those who will not be with Christ in eternity do not truly pertain to his body he said, "Now they are in one, still they will not always be in one. He is indeed that servant called to mind in the Gospel, of whom when the Lord will have come he will divide him and place him in the lot of the hypocrites."

---

[53] *De Corrept. et Gratia*, cap. 9.

[54] lib. 3 cap. 32.

## CHAPTER VIII
*On Those who are not Perfect*

IT can easily be proven that there are imperfect men in the Church, against the opinion of the Pelagians and the Anabaptists. If those who had any imperfection were not in the Church, then there never would have been nor would be any Church on earth. For with the exception of Christ and the Blessed Virgin (who by themselves do not make the Church), there is no one, even if he were very holy in this life, who does not have some venial sins, even though they do not abolish justice nor make man an enemy of God, as the Pelagians thought. That is particularly taught in Scripture. "You forgave the impiety of my sin, for this every holy man will pray to you in due season."[1] What is the "for this," except for this remission of sin? Furthermore, the holy man is a man, and he still has something that he begs to be remitted him. In the Old Testament it says, "For there is no man who shall not sin,"[2] and again, "The just man falls seven times a day and rises again,"[3] and, "No man is so just on earth that he does good and does not sin."[4] In Matthew all are bid to

---

[1] Ps. 31(32).

[2] 3 Kings (1 Kings) 8:46.

[3] Proverbs 24:16.

[4] Eccles. 7:21.

say, "Forgive us our sins." James says, "We have all offended in many things."⁵ and "If we will have said that we do not have sin, we deceive ourselves and we do not have the truth."⁶ Such testimonies are certainly so clear that they hardly need any explanation.

Likewise the Council of Miletus defines in canons 7 and 8 that the just say "forgive our sins," not just out of humility but also in truth—not just for others but even for themselves.

The Fathers witness the same thing. St. Cyprian said, "Whoever says he is without fault is either proud or stupid."⁷ St. Gregory Nazianzen said, "To be free from every sin altogether is something God constituted above the mode of human nature."⁸ St. Ambrose said, "The just man cannot deny this because no man is without sin."⁹ St. John Chrysostom says, "The Church is not constituted from the perfect but contains those given over both to industry and sluggishness."¹⁰ St. Jerome said, "I concede there are just men, but I do not agree they are without any sin."¹¹ In book 3 of the same work, Jerome proves this same thing from the whole matter, when he at length

---

⁵ James 3:2.

⁶ 1 John 1:6.

⁷ *de Eleemosyna.*

⁸ Orat. 2, in Iulian.

⁹ Serm. 16 in Psal. 16.

¹⁰ in Psal. 39.

¹¹ *Contra Pelagionaos*, lib. 2.

admits that a man can go a very brief time without sin, but not long.

St. Augustine teaches that a man can live without any sin by a singular privilege from God, but really there is no one who lives or has lived thus but Christ.[12] He says the same thing in *de natura et gratia,* cap. 34, where he also exempts the Blessed Virgin, and in epist. 89, 95 and in the whole book on perfect justice, and finally in book 1 against the two Pelagian epistles, cap. 14. "There is no one in the Church that could rightly be ordained a minister, if the Apostle would have said if anyone is free from sin, where he said free from crime; or if he had said those having no sin when he said those having no crime. To be sure, there are many baptized faithful that are not guilty of a crime, but in this life I say there is no one without sin." St. Gregory the Great said that in this life there are many not guilty of a crime, but no one that lives without sin.[13]

There are many arguments to the contrary, but they do not all need to be answered here. Those which are advanced to prove that any sin destroys justice, or that a man can live without any sin, do not lack an answer since a little later we will show that the best and the most wicked men are in the Church. There are only two arguments proper to this place. One is from the Canticles, "You are all beautiful, my beloved, and there is no stain in

---

[12] *De Spiritu et litera*, cap. ult.

[13] Moral., lib. 21, cap. 9.

you,"[14] and the other, "That he might show the glorious Church to himself, having no stain or blemish, or anything of this kind."[15] That passage must be understood about the Church, as the sixth Council of Toledo teaches in its first chapter, explaining the confession of faith.

I respond: To the first, it is either understood on the Church by reason of only one part (*i.e.* by reason of just souls), or on the perfect soul, which I would prefer to argue. For the just soul is called all beautiful, either through hyperbole (which is familiar to lovers), or because the just and perfect soul lacks mortal sins, which properly leave behind a stain and avoids venial sins as much as it is permitted for human frailty to do so, and if it were to commit such it will soon labor to blot them out. Even if it is not immaculate simply, still it is immaculate for the state of this life, as Augustine explains in his book on the perfection of justice. In this way no one is perfect in this life absolutely, and nevertheless many in the Scriptures are said to be perfect because they were such for the state of this life. In Genesis it says, "Noah was a just man and also perfect,"[16] and, "Let all of us who are perfect be of this mind."[17] Nay more they are also called Immaculate who lack venial sins, "And I will be Immaculate with him."[18]

---

[14] Cantic. 4:7.

[15] Ephes. 5:27.

[16] Gen. 5:9.

[17] Philipp. 3:15.

[18] Psal. 17[18]:24.

"Blessed are the immaculate on the way."[19] "He chose us in himself, that we might be holy and immaculate in truth."[20]

I say to the second argument that a) it can be understood about the Church, not as it now is but as it will be after the resurrection, as St. Jerome explains it,[21] as well as St. Augustine,[22] and St. Bernard.[23] The Council of Toledo is not opposed to this either, because even if the Council understood those words on the Church in this time, nevertheless it did not define it. Still, I say b) it is more probable that the Apostle spoke about the Church of this time but attributed it through a figure of speech to the whole Church, which agrees with one part of it. For those who are now the just in the Church, that are glorious through the beauty of grace which is an innate glory, who are the ones without stain, as it was expressed a little earlier, without blemish, because they have been renewed through baptism; they have laid aside the old man and put on the new, the blemishes are signs of the old man. So all understand this passage apart from the Council of Toledo that has already been cited, such as Chrysostom, Jerome and Theophylactus in their commentaries on those passages.

---

[19] Psal. 118 [119]:1.

[20] Ephesians I:4.

[21] *in Hieremiae*, cap. 31.

[22] de Perfect. Iustit., et other places.

[23] Serm. 3, *de festo omnium Sanctorum*.

## CHAPTER IX
### *On Great Sinners*

OREOVER, in the one true and Catholic Church of Christ there are not only imperfect men but even great sinners, and not only secret ones but even manifest ones. This is proved against the error of the Novationists, Donatists and Confessionists. First, it is proved from the parables of the Gospels on the chaff, on the net, on the nuptial dinner, the ten virgins and on the sheepfold that we cited above, with which Catholics once so refuted the Donatists that the latter found no way to escape them, as Augustine relates in his short work on the conference with the Donatists, explaining the conference of the third day.

Besides, there are other very clear passages. In Matthew it says, "If your brother might have sinned against you, go correct him, etc. If he will not hear you, speak to the Church, if he will not hear the Church, let him be to you just as a pagan and a publican."[1] Here it cannot be denied that the discourse is on the true Church, for Christ speaks about his Church and in this Church it is certain that sinners are discovered, even such sinners who often are not mended by fraternal correction, nor by the application of two witnesses, and still they remain in the Church until they are thrown out of the Church by the

---

[1] Matthew 18:17.

judgment of a prelate. We also see in Matthew that the Lord commands in regard to wicked overseers that we should do what they say but not what they do.[2] Next the Lord describes a wicked overseer who strikes the converted, eats and drinks with the drunkards, and he says, "The Lord will come on a day which he hopes not and he will divide him and place his share with that of the hypocrites."[3] Hilary, Jerome, Chrysostom and others teach on that passage that it is in regard to those in charge of the Church. Likewise Paul says that he writes to the Church of God, which is in Corinth, and soon he adds, "It has been shown to me that there are contentions among you."[4] And in chapter 5, "fornication is heard of among you and such fornication that is not known among the nations, so that a man has the wife of his father."[5] What will they say here? That it is not the true Church? But the Apostle calls it the Church of God; that it was not a very great and manifest sinner? Yet the Apostle says it. That he was not in that Church? But the Apostle commands that they expel him through excommunication. "Let him be taken away from your midst, etc."

Additionally, St. John writes in the book of the Apocalypse to the seven Churches of Asia,[6] and condemns individuals for no light matters. As Augustine remarks,

---

[2] Matthew 23.

[3] Matthew 24:50.

[4] 1 Cor. 1:11.

[5] 1 Cor. 5:1.

[6] Apocalypse 2 et 3.

John not only condemns the Churches, but even the Bishops, signified by the Angel of the Church of Sardis, "You have the name which you could live, but you are dead, be watchful, etc."[7] Add that in the time of the Old Testament the people of God never lacked very serious sins, and still we never read that Moses or Samuel or other Prophets who lived in different times, or Mary, Anna, Elizabeth, Simeon, Zachariah, John the Baptist and the other just, whom the Lord discovered in the people of the Jews, separated themselves from the other very evil men in regard to the temple, altar, sacrifices and other things which are of religion, hence, the good and the bad remained in the same congregation. St. Augustine duly urges this very argument.[8]

Secondly it is proven from the testimony of the Catholic Church in St. Augustine's time. For Augustine relates a famous conference held in Carthage among 306 Catholic Bishops (of which he himself was one), with 296 Donatist Bishops. Augustine indicates that there were that many on the first day, then in the conference on the third day the Donatists were compelled to admit that the good and the bad are in the Church, and the Catholics advanced the parables on the net gathering the good and bad fish, but the Donatists still said those who are secretly wicked are in the Church, just as in the net while it is in the sea the good fish are not known from the bad, but on the shore they will soon be separated. The Catholic Bishops

---

[7] lib. 2, *contra Parmenianum*, cap. 10.

[8] *Breviculo, loc. cit.*

responded to this that on that account the Church is compared to a seine, in which the chaff is discerned from the grain, nay more the chaff appears more than the grain. Further they argued that in the ark of Noah, after the exit of the raven (which signifies heretics), the clean and unclean animals still clearly remained in the ark.

Augustine also adds that when the Donatists misrepresented Catholics as making two Churches, one on earth which would have the good and evil but the other in heaven which had none but the good, then the Catholics responded that they do not make two Churches but distinguish two periods of the Church, "They said that there is now one and the same holy Church, but later it will be otherwise, now it is mixed with the wicked, then it is not going to have them just as there are not two Christs because Christ was at one point mortal and then immortal." Such things must also be noted against the Confessionists and the Calvinists who create two Churches.

Thirdly, it is proven from the testimonies of the Fathers. Cyprian said, "Neither faith nor our charity ought to be impeded; just because we discern that cockle is in the Church, is no reason to depart from the Church."[9] St. Gregory Nazianzen compares the Church to a vast sea monster composed of many such creatures, that is from the great, the small, wild, meek, etc. to show that the greatest labor is that of Bishops who ought to rule so many kinds of men, the perfect and the imperfect, the

---

[9] lib. 3, *epist. 3 ad Maximum.*

good and the bad.[10] St. John Chrysostom says many similar things on the sins of those who are ruled by Bishops.[11] Commenting on Psalm 39 (40), on that verse, *They are multiplied over the hairs of my head,* he said: "The whole Church is certainly not constituted from the perfect, but it also has those who from laziness give themselves over to inaction, and embrace a soft and dissolute life, and gladly serve their desires, at length both the former and the latter announce that it is one body from one person."

Jerome says, "The ark of Noah was a type of the Church, just as in it were all kinds of animals so also in the Church there are men of all kinds of nations and morals, just in the ark there were leopards, goats and wolves as well as sheep, so also in the Church there are the just and sinners, *i.e.,* vessels of gold and silver along with those of wood and clay."[12] Augustine says, "We affirm that both the good and the wicked are in the Catholic Church, but just as the grain and the chaff."[13] Fulgentius says, "Firmly hold and in nowise doubt the threshing floor of God is the Catholic Church, and within it even to the end of the world it contains the chaff mixed with grain, that is, the wicked are mixed with the good in

---

[10] Orat. 1, *Apologetica.*

[11] lib. 3 *de sacerdotio.*

[12] *Dialogus contra Luciferianos.*

[13] *Tract. 6 in Ioannem. cf. Retract.,* lib. 2, cap. 18; liber *post collationem,* cap. 7 et 20; *de Unitate Ecclesiae,* cap. 13; *De Civitate Dei,* lib. 18, cap. 4, 9, and other places.

the communion of the Sacraments."[14] St. Gregory also teaches the wicked are in the Church and proves it with many arguments.[15]

Lastly, it is proved from reason. For if only the good were in the Church then the Sacrament of Penance would be in vain since it is administered only to those who are in the Church. Besides no man would know for certain who was or was not in the Church, since it would be uncertain who was really good or not. Likewise, if some prelate were to sooner or later fall into sin then he would no longer be in the Church and hence no longer a prelate and therefore it would not be necessary to obey him any longer; just the same if his subjects sooner or later would sin, they would no longer be in the flock and therefore it would be lawful for the pastors to omit their care; but from such confusion great disturbance would arise.

Still they object; 1) from the Scripture: "He will not add beyond that he should pass over to the uncircumcised and the unclean.... Withdraw, withdraw, go out from there, do not touch anyone polluted, go out from their midst."[16] The Apostle explains this passage thus, "I will receive you, says the Lord."[17] Therefore, God does not receive anyone in his Church except those who separate themselves from the unclean and sinners. Paul gives the reason (*loc. cit.*) saying, "What participation does justice have with

---

[14] *de fide ad Petrum*, cap. 43.

[15] Hom. 11 et 38 in Evangelia.

[16] Isaiah 52:11.

[17] 2 Cor. 6:18.

iniquity? What compact does Christ have with Belial?" In 1 Corinthinas he says, "One bread and one body we are many."[18] But bread is only effected from grain, not chaff and grain. In Romans he says, "Whoever does not have the spirit of Christ is not of him,"[19] and, "In the one spirit we are all baptized into one body."[20] Therefore, whoever does not have the spirit is a sinner, and not a member of Christ. If one were to say he is not a living member but still he is a member, on the other hand because he is a dead member he is not a member except by a figure of speech, therefore he is not a true member and thus not one at all.

St. Augustine responds to the first argument.[21] The Church triumphant is understood in that passage, "he will not add more that he should pass over to the uncircumcised and unclean." What is added, "Recede, go out, etc.," is understood on the separation which ought to happen in the soul and the dead but not in the corporal separation from the same temple and Sacraments, etc.

But Cyril of Jerusalem says it better when he comments on this passage of Isaiah (and it does not seem that Jerome disagrees). He teaches that it is according to the historic sense, and it is a question of the temporal persecution of the Jews that the sense might be when you return from captivity an addition should not be made, *i.e.*

---

[18] 1 Cor. 10:17.

[19] Romans 8:9.

[20] 1 Cor. 12.

[21] lib. *contra Donatistas post collationem,* cap. 8 et 20, et in *Breviculo Collationis tertia diei.*

for a long time, some infidel persecutor shall pass through your lands, devastating them, but according to the mystical sense it is a question of the Church, and Isaiah foretold that the gates of hell would not prevail against it. For the uncircumcised and the unclean are principally the enemies of the Church, that is the demons. For equal reasoning it follows that, "recede, recede, etc." according to the historic sense is understood about the Jews whom Isaiah exhorts go out from Babylon since the time of captivity was limited; but according to the mystical sense it is understood about Christians who ought, after Baptism, to be separated from the bodies, temples and sacrifices of unbelievers, along with their spouses and all the rest which also pertain to religion. And St. Paul understands this passage in that manner when he says speaks not on the commerce with certain sinners, but only with the infidels, "Do not take up the yoke with infidels, what share do the faithful have with the unbelievers? What union is there with the temple of God and idols?"

To what was said on the one bread, which is from the wheat alone, I respond: the similitudes do not agree in everything. This similitude consists of the bread and of the Church, as Cyprian and Irenaeus explain,[22] just as one bread is made from many grains through water, so also from many men through the waters of Baptism, or through the Holy Spirit, who is also called water,[23] one people of God is made. No man is in the Church who has

---

[22] epist. 6, lib. 1 *ad Magnum*, Irenaeus, lib. 3 cap. 19.

[23] Ezechiel 36.

not been baptized and does not participate in either an internal or external gift of the Holy Spirit. Although it is also not true that bread consists of wheat alone. Meanwhile either from negligence or from their malice, were those who make bread to mix in even a grain of chaff, just as often in wine from the malice of the sellers it is mixed with water. Next, the same is shown from the very words of Paul in 1 Corinthians 10:17 when he says, "We are one bread and one body, we who participate in one bread." But the good and the bad participated in the one bread, otherwise Paul would not have argued that some communicate unworthily.[24]

To the last point I say that the wicked are not living members of the body of Christ and the Scriptures themselves signify this. To that which is added, that they are members by a figure of speech, etc., it is usually conceded by many men that the wicked are not true members of the body of the Church, nor simply, but only according to something and by a figure of speech, such as Juan Torquemada[25], and he tries to show it from Alexander of Hales, Hugh and St. Thomas. Pedro de Soto, Melchior Cano and others also teach the same thing, even if they say the wicked are not true members, just the same they say they are truly in the Church, or in the body of the Church and are faithful, that is Christians simply. For not only are members in the body, but also the humors, the teeth, the hair and other things. And faithful or

---

[24] 1 Cor. 11:27.

[25] Lib. 1, cap. 57.

Christians are not called such from charity, but from faith or by the profession of faith. But if that is so, it follows that a bad Pope is not the head of the Church, and bishops, if they will be bad, are not the heads of their Churches. For the head is not a humor, or a hair, but a member and certainly a special one; but this is against the Council of Constance wherein the error of Jan Hus was condemned which asserted that a bad shepherd is only a shepherd by a figure of speech. It also condemned his error which asserted that a bad prelate is not truly a prelate.[26]

Consequently, I respond that members can be considered in two ways: a) as there are certain matters according to themselves or according to their essence and substance; b) as they are operative instruments, e.g., a man's eye and a cow's eye, as they are certain substances they are different in regard to species, by reason of different souls. But as operative instruments, they are species of the same thing because they have the same object.

So, I say a bad Bishop, priest, teacher, etc., are dead members and so they are not true members of the body of Christ in so far as it attains to the purpose of the member, as it is a certain part of the living body, nevertheless they are truly members by reason of the instrument, i.e. the Pope and the Bishops are true heads, the Doctors true eyes, or a true tongue of this body, etc., and the reason is because they are constituted living members by charity,

---

[26] In quo sess. 15 damnatur error XXII; XXX error.

which the impious lack. But the operative instruments are constituted either by the power of order or of jurisdiction, which can also exist without grace. For even if in the natural body a dead member cannot be an instrument of operation, still it can, in the mystical body. In a natural body the work depends upon the goodness of the instrument, because the soul cannot operate well unless it does through good instruments, nor can it exercise works of life except through living instruments. The soul of this body, *i.e.*, the Holy Spirit works equally well through good and bad instruments, as well as living and dead, etc.

The second objection. The Church is called "Holy" in the Creed, therefore it is constituted by none but the holy. Those who make this objection will say that the response that the Church is called holy because one part of the Church is holy does not suffice. For then, the Church could also be called sinful because one part, nay more the greater part is sinful.

I respond: The Church is truly said to be holy because all the things that pertain to her constitution are holy. First baptism, which no man denies is holy. Secondly, Christian profession, that is the profession of faith, as well as of morals, doctrines and Christian precepts. It is certain that she is holy and that only she is holy by this profession since the profession of the Jews, Turks, Heathen and heretics is not holy; and only that of Christians is. Thirdly, the union of members among themselves and with the head, at least the external head, and in regard to those things which pertain to religion is also certainly holy. She is called holy on account of the saints that she has, but she ought not be called sinful on that account since a denomination is made from its better part. Besides, it is proper for the Church to have saints because she alone truly has holy people, but to have wicked men is not proper to the Church, for that agrees with other bodies as well. Next, she is called holy because she is wholly consecrated to God and because Christ her head is the holy of holies.

The third objection. He who does not have the Church as a mother does not have God as a Father, as St. Cyprian teaches; likewise one who does not have the Church as a mother does not have God as a father. But none of the wicked have God as a father, "For those who are urged by the Spirit of God, these are the sons of God,"[27] and it is said to the wicked, "You are from your father the devil."[28] and again, "In this you are manifested as sons of God and sons of the devil, everyone who is not just is not from God." Therefore, only the good have the Church as a mother, so only the good are in the Church.

I respond with St. Augustine,[29] that the name of "son" is received in three ways in the Scriptures. In one way sons are called according to production, whether that is properly by generation, or creation, or regeneration; thus Christ the Lord is properly called the Son of God because he was generated by God the Father, all men also are sons by reason of creation. "Is he not your father who made

---

[27] Romans 8.

[28] John 8.

[29] contra Adimantum, cap. 5.

and created you?"[30] Still by reason of a new regeneration all sons are called just, and only just as in the places we have cited, Romans 8 and 1 John 3. Secondly, some are called sons by reason of imitation, just as the Apostle calls the sons of Abraham those who imitate the faith of Abraham,[31] and again, "Love your enemies and do good to those who hate you that you might be sons of your father, etc."[32] And in this way only the good are sons of God, for all the wicked are sons of the devil, as it says in John 8 and 1 John 3. Thirdly, they are called sons by reason of doctrine, this is why the Apostle calls the Corinthians sons,[33] because he taught them the Gospel, and again he says, "My children, whom I give birth to a second time until Christ will have been formed in you."[34] In this way all who are in the Church are sons of God and the Church, because they adhere to the true doctrine of God and the Church, but they can still be good and wicked. This is why Isaiah says, "I nurtured the children and raised them up, and they hoped in me,"[35] and the Canticles declare, "My beloved is among the daughters as a lily among thorns." There, Christian souls are called daughters, but wicked.

With these being noted we respond to the argument. If it is a question of the sons of doctrine, the assumption is

---

[30] Deut. 32.

[31] Gal. 4; Rom. 4.

[32] Matthew 5.

[33] 1 Cor. 4.

[34] Galatians 4.

[35] Isaiah 1.

false, for it is not true that only the just are sons of God if only the reason of doctrine is considered; but if it is a question of the sons of God by regeneration or imitation, the last consequent is bad, therefore only the good are in the Church; for not only the sons but the servants also, although these do not remain in the house for ever, the sons remain forever,[36] and this is the mind of St. Cyprian. He did not mean that in the Church there are none but the sons, but there are not any sons outside the Church, just as there are not any good men outside, although there might be evil ones within. He meant to terrify heretics and schismatics, and to warn them to not think they can be either good, or sons outside the Church.

The fourth objection is also from St. Cyprian, when he says, "Only the peaceful and harmonious dwell in the Church, as God who makes those in unity dwell in his home, as it is in the Psalms through the Holy Spirit."[37] Thus, sinners who fight and make contentions with others are not in the Church."

I respond: Cyprian does not speak on every peace, but on that which is properly said to be opposed to schismatics. Besides, there can be other dissensions in the Church and in fact one often finds them, as Cyprian himself witnesses in his sermon *de Lapsis*, where among other sins, he also places among men in the Church who separated themselves from pertinacious hatred for each other.

---

[36] John VIII.

[37] lib. 1, epist. 6 ad Magnum.

The fifth argument is from St. John Chrysostom and Theophylactus commenting on 2 Timothy 2, where they say, "In a great house there are golden vessels, etc." They say that this cannot be understood about the Church but about the world, because in the Church there are no vases but gold and silver.

I respond: They do not deny that the wicked can be in the Church but they say it is not necessary that they be in the Church because when the Apostle says that in a great house there are golden, silver, clay and wooden vessels, it is known that all these are necessary lest someone might think the Church cannot exist without the wicked. So these Fathers say that by the term "house", not the Church but the world should be understood since the Church does not need the wicked, nay more when it will be in its best state, *i.e.* in heaven, it will have no wicked members. Yet the world is furnished with the wicked, not *per se* but *per accidens*, if there were no wicked men then the patience of the just would not be exercised in this world, nor the justice of God.

The sixth argument is taken from St. Jerome in his commentary on Ephesians 5. He says on the subjection of the Church to Christ, "The Church of Christ is glorious, having no stain, no blemish, nor anything of this sort. A sinner or anyone stained with filth cannot be said to be of the Church nor subject to Christ."

I respond: Jerome means that the wicked cannot be said to be in that part of the Church that contains only the perfect. He explains in his commentary on Galatians 1 on that verse, "Paul, an Apostle, ... to the Churches of

Galatia," he means to explain how the words of the Apostle embrace in themselves those who now seem to praise all the Churches, then reproach and rebuke them; he says the Church is received in a two-fold sense, *i.e.* not that there are two Churches, but on the one diverse-mode the Scriptures speak; sometimes Scripture attributes that which is proper to the perfect to the whole Church, namely, that it lacks stain or blemish, and sometimes that which is proper to the imperfect, such as to sin and the need for correction. When the Church is praised it must be taken in respect to that part which contains the perfect, when it is rebuked then to that which contains the imperfect.

The seventh argument is from Pacianus, who says, "In the Church there is no stain or blemish because sinners are not in the Church until they will have done penance for their prior life, and after that are cleansed."[38]

I respond: He does not speak about all sinners, but only on sinners who fell into heresy, for before that he had said the Church lacks stain and blemish because she lacks heresy.

The eighth argument is taken from St. Augustine who says, "But by this, even without the knowledge of the Church, on account of the wicked and polluted conscience, those damned by Christ are not in the body of Christ, which is the Church, because Christ cannot have

---

[38] Epist. 3 ad Sympronianum.

damned members."[39] He holds similar things in other places.[40]

I respond, on account of these citations, not only Brenz and Calvin, but even some Catholics imagine that there are two Churches, but they really imagine it, for neither the Scriptures nor Augustine ever call to mind two Churches, but only one. Certainly in the short conference with the Donatists, where they falsely asserted that Catholics make two Churches (one for the good and another which contains the good with the wicked), the Catholic side responded that they never dreamed of two Churches, but only distinguish parts, or times of the Church. Parts, because on the one hand the good pertain to the Church, and on the other the wicked, since the good are the interior part, just like the soul of the Church, and the wicked are the exterior part, just like the body. Then they gave the example concerning the interior man and the exterior, which are not two men but one part of the same man.

With regard to times, they spoke distinguishing on the one hand the Church today, and on another the Church after the resurrection; today it has good and wicked men, after the resurrection it will not have any but the good. They also placed the example of Christ, who is always the same but nevertheless was mortal and passible before his resurrection, but afterwards immortal and impassible. St.

---

[39] *Contra Cresconium*, lib.2, cap. 21.

[40] *Contra Petilianum*, lib. 2, cap. ult.; *de Baptismo*, lib. 4, cap. 3, lib. 6, cap. 3, lib. 7, cap. 49, 50, 51; *de Unitate Ecclesiae*, cap. ult.; *Doctrina Christiana*, lib. 3, cap. 32.

Augustine often confirms the same doctrine in other places and explains it with various similitudes. Against the Donatists he says that the good are in the house of God, which is the Church, so that the house of God might be built upon living stones, while the wicked are in the same house, but these, nevertheless are not the house.[41] In the last chapter of his book *On the Unity of the Church*, he says that the wicked are cut off from the Church in spirit but not in body; in other words they pertain to the Church as to the exterior man, but not to the interior. In *Doctrina Christiana*, while explaining the verse in the Canticles, "I am black but beautiful, just as a cedar tent, just as the skin of Solomon," he notes that it was not said "I was black and I am beautiful," but "I *am* black and beautiful," because the Church now is one and the same, black just as a cedar tent, on account of the sinners which she has in her, and at the same time beautiful, just as the skin of Solomon, *i.e.*, just as the halls of a king, because of the good which she has in her.[42]

Augustine says the same thing on the epistle of John, where he teaches that the wicked are indeed in the body of the Church, not as members, but as corrupted humors which remain in the breast and really are in the body, and nevertheless are also truly separated from the members of the body. From the latter the response is made that when Augustine says the wicked are not in the Church, it ought

---

[41] *Contra Donatistas*, lib. 7, cap. 51.

[42] lib. 3, cap. 32.

to be understood to be in that way in which the good are, that is, they are not living members of the body.

But one might object that St. Augustine also teaches that only the saints are the Church, which is founded upon the rock, and to which the keys of the kingdom were given,[43] and about which it was said if he will not hear the Church, let him be to you just as a heathen and a publican.

I respond: Augustine meant nothing other than that all privileges which were conceded to the universal Church by God were conceded on account of the saints alone for the advantage and benefit of those who obtain eternal salvation. Otherwise, Augustine frequently repeats the same thing; wicked Christians advantageously administer the Sacraments and hence rule men, loose them, bind them, etc. Consequently,[44] he compares evil ministers to a stony channel, through which water passes to the garden, and although it acquires no advantage for itself, nevertheless it is the cause for grass and flowers to be born and grow in the garden.[45]

The ninth argument is of the Lutheran Centuriators of Magdeburg. They try to show that there are two Churches, one of the good and one of the wicked.[46] They distinguish the justice of the disciples in Matthew 5 from the justice of the Pharisees, in Matthew 6 of the pious

---

[43] *de Baptismo*, lib. 3, cap. 18, lib. 1, cap. 21 et 22, lib. 6, cap. 3, lib. 7 cap. 51.

[44] Tract. 5 *in Ioannem*.

[45] *C.f. Contra Parmenianum*, lib. 2, cap. 10 et 11.

[46] *Centur.* 1, lib. 1, cap. 4, col. 171.

from the hypocrites, in Matthew 7 the body of wayfarers traveling on the narrow path from the body of those going through the broad road, and in the same place they distinguish the house founded upon the rock from the one founded upon sand. Moreover, they say it is certain that the Church of the wicked is not one holy Catholic Church, therefore the true Church of Christ only embraces the good.

I respond: Two Churches are not distinguished in any of those passages, but only different qualities of those who are in one and the same Church. Just the same, Matthew 13 distinguishes good fish from bad fish, and still they are in the same net, which signifies the Church. Thus, they are also in the same Church who make the profession of the same faith and are in the communication of the same Sacraments, indeed they are those who walk on the broad road of vices, just as those who walk on the narrow path of virtue; just as those who are truly pious and those who are hypocrites; and those who follow the justice of the Pharisees as well as those who follow the justice of the Apostles. Lastly, there are some just as a house founded upon a rock, and those who are like a house founded upon sand. For in this passage it does not signify two Churches, as if we wanted to make as many Churches as there are men, for the Lord says, "Therefore, everyone who hears my words and does them, he will be compared to a wise man who built his house upon the rock, etc."

The tenth argument. If the body of Christ is the Church they cannot be parts and members of this body, among whom Christ works nothing. For he works nothing in the impious and the hypocrites; as a result, they are not of the same sort as those who can pertain to the Church of Christ. Likewise, it is altogether fitting to distinguish the kingdom of Christ from the kingdom of the devil, but all the impious pertain to the kingdom of the devil, therefore, only the pious pertain to the kingdom of Christ, which is the Church.

I respond: It is not necessary that Christ work something in all his members, for there are some dead members, some shriveled, which only adhere to the rest by an external connection. Moreover, if the kingdom of Christ is distinct from the kingdom of the devil, still the same men can pertain to each kingdom: those who are provided with bad morals yet persevere in the Catholic faith, and the union with the other faithful, they pertain to the kingdom of Christ insofar as the profession of faith. Yet, they pertain to the kingdom of the devil in respect to the perversity of morals. For this reason Augustine says the impious who are in the Church are sons and foreigners; sons on account of the form of piety, but foreigners on account of the loss of virtues.[47]

---

[47] In Psal. 47(48).

# CHAPTER X
## *On Secret Infidels*

ASTLY, it remains to speak of secret infidels, *i.e.* those who have neither internal faith nor any Christian virtue, but nevertheless profess the Catholic faith due to some temporal advantage and mix with the true faithful by the communion of the Sacraments. Both the Confessionists and Calvinists teach that such men in no way pertain to the true Church, and even some Catholics, one of whom is Juan Torquemada,[1] although this author perhaps meant nothing other than that they require faith for someone can be said to be united by an internal union to the body of Christ, which is the Church, which would be very true.

Nevertheless, we follow the manner of speaking of a great many authors who teach that they who are joined with the remaining faithful only by an external profession are true parts and even members of the Church but withered and dead.[2]

---

[1] Lib. 4, *de Ecclesia*, par. 2, cap. 20.

[2] Thomas Waldens, tomus I, lib. 2 cap. 9, nu. 10, et cap. 11, num. 5; John Driedo, *de Ecclesiasticis Scripturis et dogmatibus*, lib. 4, cap. 2, par. 2; Pedro de Soto *Confessio Catholica*, (which was opposed to the Augsburg Confession), cap. de Ecclesia, et cap. de Conciliis, et in Apologia pro eadem Confessione par. 1, cap. 11; Cardinal Hosius, *contra Prolegomena Brentii*, lib. 3; Melchior Cano, lib. 4 de Locis Theologicis, cap. ult. ad

1) This opinion can be demonstrated from those words of John: "And now many have become Antichrists, they went out from us, but they were not from us; for if they were from us they would have remained with us."[3] John speaks in this place on heretics, whom he calls Antichrists, and he says that before they went out, they were not from us, *i.e.* they were not Catholics in spirit and will but heretics and Antichrists, and still they went out from us because if they were not from us, in spirit and will, nevertheless they were by external profession; but after they betrayed themselves and broke out into open schism, they already ceased to be from us in every way.

And, although at some time St. Augustine explained those words, "They were not from us," about predestination, still in his commentary on this passage, he explains they are about secret heretics. He speaks thus: "All heretics, all schismatics, went out from us, that is, they went out from the Church, but they would not have gone out if they were from us, namely, they went out from the Church, but they would not have gone out if they were from us. Before they went out, therefore, they were not from us, if before they went out they were not from us. Many are inside that did not go out, and yet they are Antichrists.... And those who are inside are certainly in the body of our Lord Jesus Christ since he still takes care of his own body; but health will not be restored except in the resurrection of the dead; thus they are in the

___

argumentum XII.

[3] 1 John 2:19.

body of Christ in the same way as bad humors. For, when they are vomited then the body is relieved; thus even the wicked, when they go out, then the Church is relieved and when she vomits them out, and the body casts them out, she says these humors go out from me, but they were not from me. Why were they not from me? They were not cut from my flesh but pressed from my breast when they were present there."[4] He explains it in the same way in other places,[5] which we will present below.

2) Next the same thing is proven from the testimonies of those Fathers who teach in a common consensus that those who are outside the Church have no authority or jurisdiction in the Church.[6]

Moreover, right reason manifestly teaches the same thing: By what arrangement can it be devised or imagined that one might have jurisdiction and hence be the head of the Church, who is not a member of the Church? Whoever heard of a head which was not a member? Moreover it is certain, whatever one or another might think, a secret heretic, if he might be a Bishop, or even the Supreme Pontiff, does not lose jurisdiction, nor dignity, or

---

[4] Tract. 3, *in epistolam Ioannis.*

[5] De Baptismo lib. 3, cap. 18, Tract. 61 in Ioannem.

[6] Cyprian, lib. 1, epist. 6, lib. 2 epist. 1; Optatus, *contra Parmenianum,* lib. 1; Ambrose *de poenitentia,* lib. 1, cap. 2; Jerome *dioalogus contra Luciferianos*; Augustine, *in Enchiridio,* cap. 65; Pope Celestine *epistola ad Clerum Constantinopolitanum, epistola ad Ioannem Antiochenum, c.f.* 1 Tomo Concilii Ephesini, cap. 18 et 19, cited by Nicholas I in his epistle to the Emperor Michael.

the name of the head in the Church, until either he separates himself publicly from the Church, or being convicted of heresy is separated against his will; for this reason, Celestine and Nicholas say (*loc. cit.*) that a heretical Bishop, to the extent that he began to preach heresy, could bind and loose no one although without a doubt if he had already conceived the error, were it before he began to preach publicly, he could still bind and loose. The fact is likewise confirmed from the canon *Audivimus*, 24, q. 1, where we read: "But if he will have devised a new heresy in his heart, to the extent that he begins to preach such things, he can condemn no man." Besides, if it were the case that secret heretics could have no jurisdiction, every act that depends upon jurisdiction would be rendered uncertain, which would disturb the universal Church in no small measure. Therefore, now if he who is not in the Church cannot have authority in the Church and a secret heretic can have it, and at some point really has authority in the Church, certainly a secret heretic can be in the Church.

3) The same thing is proven from Origen, Augustine and Gregory. Origen says, "Even here in Jerusalem (*i.e.* in the Church), there are some Jebusites who are perverse in their faith and deeds."[7] There is no doubt whether he spoke about secret heretics, for he adds: "Nor do we speak about those who are manifestly and evidently guilty enough to be expelled from the Church."

---

[7] *Homil. 21 in Iosue.*

Augustine says, "The enemies of this fraternal charity are either clearly outside or seem to be inside, as pseudochristians and Antichrists, for after they have discovered opportunities, then they go out. But even if they lack opportunities, although they seem to be inside, they have been separated by the invisible bond of charity."[8] When Augustine says these things about secret heretics, that they seem to be in the Church, he does not mean they are not really in the Church, but that they are not in the manner in which they seem. They seem to be united by an internal and external bond with the other members but still they are not united except by an external bond. For if they were not really inside in any way but only seemed to be, for equal reasoning they would not truly go out when they clearly betray themselves, but would only seem to go out.

Moreover, Augustine says they go out after they have found opportunities, and he adds they were separated even before they went out, but from the invisible bond of charity, not from the external communion of the Church. What Augustine says later in the same work[9] ought to be understood in the same way. There, he says that secret heretics are separated so that they may be judged, even if they do not go out. He speaks on the internal separation, not on the external, and this is not proper in Augustine to secret heretics but to all sinners, whom Augustine affirms are not in the body of the Church, as is clear from the

---

[8] *de Baptismo*, lib. 3, cap. 18.

[9] Lib.4, cap.16

chapters we cited above. Augustine continues in this place: "Wherefore, when John said they went out from us but they were not from us, he did not say they became foreigners by going out, but that they were foreigners on account of this: they declared they left." The Apostle Paul also speaks on certain men who erred concerning faith, they were in one great house, I believe that they had not yet gone out.

Augustine continues, "Even if those onl are to be alled cockle who remain in perverse error to the end, there are many grains of wheat outside, and much cockle within."[10] The sense of such words seems to be that we understand outside the Church there are many manifest heretics who at length will be converted to the true faith, and inside in the Church herself there are many secret heretics who never converted. He has the same thing in *City of God*, where he says, "He rightly called to mind that those who were going to be citizens lurked among his very enemies, just as the city of God would hold itself from their number connected in communion of the Sacraments."[11] Here it must be observed on enemies, who are outside the Church, Augustine said they are future citizens because they are merely not citizens but will be in their time. But on enemies who lurk within the Church, he does not say they are going to be enemies, but they are presently in the Church itself although, they nevertheless pertain to the number of enemies.

---

[10] Lib. 4, cap. 10.

[11] *De Civitate Dei*, lib. 1, cap. 35.

Again, when Augustine is treating on John 13, where we read Christ was present while Judas was leaving, he says, "For us, the Lord deigned to signify with his disturbance that it is necessary to tolerate false brethren even as the cockle of the Lord's field amidst the grain even to the time of the harvest, that when some pressing reason compels a separation from them before the harvest, this cannot be done without a disturbance to the Church. This disturbance of its saints by future schismatics and heretics in just the manner the Lord foretold, prefigured himself when Judas, the wicked man, made his exit, and by his departure put an end to his mixture with the wheat which had been so long tolerated; he was disturbed but not in the flesh, rather in the spirit."[12] Further on, in the same tract, he declares that Judas was one of the Lord's disciples and nevertheless bore the type of the heretic, "One from the number, but not rightly; one in species but not in virtue; by a corporal mixture but not by a spiritual bond, joined in a unity of the flesh but not a friend of the heart; ... Both are true, both from us and not from us, according to one from us, according to another not from us, according to the communion of the Sacraments from us, according to the propriety of his crimes not from us." He speaks likewise in another work, "Some men are still placed in heart on the side of the Donatists but show themselves to be with us corporally; in regard to the flesh they are inside, but in regard to the spirit outside."[13]

---

[12] Tract. 61 in Ioan.

[13] *de gestis cum Emerito*, cap.1.

Next, in his work *On Catechizing the Unlearned*, he distinguished three kinds of Christians, secret heretics, bad Catholics and good Catholics: "There are those who wish to be Christians, to either be brought into the view of men from whom they hope for agreeable temporal assistance or because they do not want to offend some that they fear. But if they are reprobate, the Church bears them, albeit for a time, just as the sand bears the chaff for a time. If they do not correct themselves and begin to be Christians on account of the coming eternal rest, then in the end they will be separated. They cannot flatter themselves that they can be in the sand with the wheat of God, because they will not be in the barn with it, rather, they will be destined for the fated fire. There are also others with better hope, but still not with lesser danger, who now fear God and do not mock the Christian name, nor enter the Church of God with a feigned heart, but hope for happiness in this life."[14] You can clearly see there, from the discussion of these two kinds of men, the first is of those who do not fear God but mock the Christian name and enter the Church with a feigned heart, and still they are in it and remain and make up the number [of Christians] and will not be separated until that clear exodus.

St. Gregory the Great, while explaining the words of Job 16:9, *My wrinkles bear witness against me*, says: "What, except the duplicitous are meant by 'wrinkles'? The wrinkles are all those who live two-faced in this life, who

---

[14] de Catechizandis Rudibus, cap. 17.

shout the faith of the holy Church loudly but deny it with their works. Without a doubt, they lie that they are faithful in a time of peace because they see the same faith honored by the powers of the world; but when the holy Church is disturbed by the gales of sudden adversity, they show themselves on the spot to be soft in a treacherous mind.... But because the Church holds even many reprobates within the fold of faith, when a time of persecution rages, she suffers these enemies whom she seemed to nourish with the words of preaching. Let it be said, therefore, 'my wrinkles bear testimony against me,' *i.e.* they rebuke me in declaration who now place themselves in the body by their duplicity and do not amend their malice. ... Even in a time of peace the holy Church suffers false brethren while there are many in her who despair of the promise of eternity and still lie that they are faithful, but when the time of malice breaks out the mendacious man lays aside what must be gainsaid, he comes before the face because he resisted the words of the true faith with a loud voice."

4) It is proven from reason and the similitude of the human body argues for that which we seek. The Church is like the human body, as the Apostle teaches in Romans 12 and 1 Cor. 12. Moreover, in the human body we see there are many different kinds of parts to the extent that some are live and feel, some are alive and do not feel, some are neither alive nor feel, which is obvious. Therefore, nothing prevents that in the Church there will be some men who have the faith and charity, as well as some who

have only faith, and some who do not even have the faith at all but merely an external union.

Next, if those who lack internal faith are not, nor can be, in the Church, there will be no further question between us and the heretics on the visibility of the Church, proportionally, (which I make much of), so many disputations of the most erudite men, which to this point have been published will be redundant. All who have written to this point object to the Lutherans and Calvinists because they make the Church invisible. I will now prove it beyond question.

The Lutherans and Calvinists establish certain visible and external signs, namely, the preaching of the word of God and the administration of the Sacraments, and they constantly teach that wherever these signs are seen there is also the true Church of Christ. Nevertheless, because they mean only the just and the pious pertain to the true Church (and no man can say for certain who might be truly just and pious among so many that outwardly wear justice and piety before them, although it is certain that in every place there are many hypocrites and false brethren), then our writers correctly conclude that the former make the Church invisible. Since, for the Lutherans and Calvinists, justice consists only in faith and the same thing is said by those who say the Church is the body of the just and the pious and the body of true believers, then who does not see that we would plainly agree with them if we were to exclude all those from the Church who do not have true faith in their heart?

For this purpose, it is necessary that it should be constituted for us—with infallible certitude—what body of men make-up the true Church of Christ, since the traditions of Scripture and clearly all dogmas depend upon the testimony of the Church; unless we were absolutely certain what is the true Church, everything will be altogether uncertain. But one cannot constitute what the true Church might be with infallible certainty if internal faith in every member or part of the Church is required. Who knows for certain in whom there is such faith? Consequently, faith (whether it is something invisible or secret) is required for someone to pertain to the Church in some way.

Some respond to this argument in two ways. Firstly, it is certain enough that the body of faithful men can be recognized, so that it could be said if the effect of faith is discerned, then the type of protestation and confession of faith is of some sort; we even say that we truly and properly see a man even though we do not see the soul except in its effects. Secondly, they add that it is not necessary for it to be easy for us to see distinctly who these men are that make the Church, rather it is enough to assign a certain body of men within which we would know for certain or at least could believe that they all pertain to the Church. Accordingly, if the universal Roman people were shown to someone in the forum or in the theater, even though some outsiders might ultimately be mixed in, truly it would be said that he saw the Roman people even if he could not discern Romans from foreigners.

But neither answer seems to satisfy, and the first is easily refuted: The recognition from the effects is not certain, rahter, conjectural. Furthermore, the example of man does not convince, for in the first place, the effects of life in man are natural and necessary, but the effects of faith are free and voluntary, hence much less certain. We could never know for sure just by looking at someone that he whom we see is a man; accordingly it can happen that when we believe we see a man we might see an Angel or a demon in human form. Certainly, Abraham, Lot, Tobit and others in the Old Testament often believed some to be men who were angels. We, however, want to have infallible certitude concerning the Church, such as we have not from man himself, but from the form and exterior colors, as well as features of the human body, by which we cannot be deceived when we look upon it.

The second answer does not satisfy for many reasons. a) Because it can happen that the number of hypocrites would so increase that there might be more secret heretics than true and perfect Catholics and no one could truly say this body is the Church of Christ, seeing that in the body which he points out, a greater part does not pertain to the Church, nor would he himself know who might be those few who make up the Church. Although, it would have to be hoped that a greater part of those who profess the faith are sincere, still that is not certain.

b) Because the whole Church would not come together in one place so that we could say for certain that in this body is the Church; rather, it has been dispersed through various places, and we might be certain on no part, or that whole part might be without the true faith; wherever we go we will always be in doubt whether we communicate with the true Church of Christ. Now, this is not opposed to what we said elsewhere, that the particular Roman Church cannot defect from the true faith,[15] for the whole Roman Church itself comes together in some place at the same time, but is gathered while spread out in different churches, which are in the city of Rome, nor do we know for certain with infallible certitude in that body, to which we by chance have approached, that all are not without true faith in heart.

c) Because it can also happen that a whole general Council might be outside the Church. How great would it be if, among so many thousands professing faith in Christ, three hundred or four hundred men, who come together in a Council, might lack the true faith? Evidently matters that are otherwise so well known, and which it is necessary that they be certain, will be called into doubt. Certainly Brenz, as we remarked in the disputation on Councils, elevates the authority of Councils for this reason, because we are not certain whether any of the Fathers had true faith in heart, and therefore were in the Church of God, for a false Church is not a column and firmament of truth, rather, only a true Church.

d) Because if we do not distinctly know who might constitute the Church, then we will be ignorant, not only as to what the Church is but where it is, or rather more where the Church hides, which is insufficient to save the

---

[15] *On the Roman Pontiff*, book IV, ch. 6.

visibility of the Church, which we will take up in the following chapter; but now let us see what some object.

Firstly, they object that faith is a foundation like the form of the Church, when we read, "Just as a good architect placed a foundation and no man can place another foundation apart from that which has been placed, which is Christ Jesus;"[16] and, "You are built upon the foundation of Apostles and Prophets in Christ Jesus the chief cornerstone."[17] "One God, one faith, one baptism."[18]

I respond: The form of the Church is not internal faith (unless we mean to have an invisible Church) but external faith, *i.e.* the confession of faith. St. Augustine teaches this very clearly,[19] and experience witnesses it. For they are admitted to the Church who profess the faith. Moreover, in those passages, faith is not said to be the form or the foundation of the Church, but the foundation of justice, or the doctrine which is in the Church. Add that the Scriptures, just as they place faith in the Church, so also do they place charity and every gift of the Holy Spirit, but no Catholic teaches that those who do not have charity and the gifts of the Holy Spirit are not in the Church.

Secondly, they object that in the definition of the Lateran Council, which is contained in the chapter *Firmiter, de summa Trinitate et fide Catholica*, there is one

---

[16] 1 Corinth. 3:10.

[17] Ephes. 2:20.

[18] Ephesians 4:5.

[19] *contra Faustum*, lib. 19, cap. 11.

universal Church of the faithful, outside of which no man is saved; to which there is a similar definition of Pope Nicholas which is contained in *de consecrat.* dist. 1, can. *Ecclesia,* the Church is a gathering of Catholics, but none are faithful and Catholic who do not have faith in their heart, even if they profess it in mouth.

I respond: These are not definitions of the Church. The Lateran Council only meant to assert that there is one Church, not to accurately describe what it might be. Moreover it addresses the Church of the faithful, because by this name the baptized Christians are distinguished both from those who are manifestly infidels and also from catechumens who are not called faithful, as we showed above. Thus, it is the same as if the Council would have said the Church of Christians is one, not many. Secondly, the name of faithful can be received for one who publicly professes the faith, and we will speak soon in the same way about the name Catholic. Thirdly, it could truly be said that the Church of the faithful, *i.e.,* of those who have true faith in heart, is one; for chiefly, the Church only gathers those who are intentionally faithful, but when some false men are mixed in who do not truly believe, that happens apart from the intention of the Church. For if she could refuse then she would never admit them, or immediately exclude those just admitted after their fall.

Thus we come to those words of Pope Nicholas, "The Church is a gathering of Catholics." We are necessarily compelled to say that they are called Catholics who profess the Catholic faith, irrespective of their internal faith; for Nicholas bids that Churches not be made, *i.e.* as he explains it, gatherings of Catholics, without the nod of the Apostolic See. Moreover it is plain that gatherings of Catholics cannot otherwise happen than by calling into one place all of those that are said to be Catholic, *i.e.* those who publicly profess that they are Catholics.

Thirdly, they object with the testimony of the Fathers, who said that heretics are not truly Christians, such as Tertullian,[20] Cyprian,[21] Athanasius,[22] and Augustine,[23] but the Church of Christ cannot be made of any but Christians, consequently, those who do not have true faith do not pertain to the Church.

I respond: Those fathers speak on manifest heretics who have the faith of Christ neither in their heart nor in their mouth. The Christian name is of profession, and they are called Christians who preserve and follow the law and faith of Christ publicly.

Fourthly, they object that before the coming of Christ, not only the Synagogue of the Jews pertained to the Church of God, but all the Gentiles as well who, though dispersed throughout the world, truly worshiped one God. From that it seems to follow that faith might be a bond of the Church and hence, he who does not have faith does not pertain to the Church.

I respond: all those, and only those, constituted the Church of God, in all ages, who had been gathered at the

---

[20] lib. *de Pudicitia.*

[21] lib. 4, epist. 2.

[22] serm. 2 *contra Arianos.*

[23] lib. *de gratia Christi*, cap. 11.

same time in confession and assertion of one faith in one God, the creator of heaven and earth, whether these were made by sacrifices, or in another mode.

The last objection. The principle reason why secret heretics are included among the members of the Church, is that it seems that it is constituted for us with infallible certitude what body of men might be the Church; but this certitude cannot be had, even if secret heretics pertain to the Church, which is confirmed by the following arguments.

a) Those who are not baptized are not members of the Church, but no man knows for certain who might be truly baptized, both because the character of Baptism is invisible, and because even when exterior Baptism is furnished, few are present to see, and consequently the rest ought to be content with human faith.

b) The Church cannot exist without Bishops and priests, as Jerome teaches.[24] But who knows for certain who might be true Bishops and priests since that depends upon the intention of the one ordaining and upon an invisible character.

c) The excommunicated are not in the Church, as we taught above, but many are secretly excommunicated, namely, excommunicated *ipso facto* by law, and not promulgated in the presence of the people, for that reason will we not be compelled to doubt when we see someone whether they may be in the Church or not?

---

[24] *Contra Luciferianos.*

d) It often happens, or certainly can happen in some places, that manifest heretics feign themselves to be Catholics, and also Jews, Turks and pagans mix themselves with the faithful, and still, either they will not be of the Church, or we will say that the Church is the body of heretics, pagans and hypocrites.

I respond to these arguments: *resp. a)* That someone might be in the body of the Church does not require the character of Baptism, but external Baptism; nor is external Baptism required to reckon someone might be in the Church, but only that he might be admitted since, if anyone asks to be admitted to the Church, it will not happen without Baptism. Nevertheless, if someone says he has been baptized, and the contrary is not certain, he shall be admitted to the other sacraments, and through this he will be of the body of the Church. Now, the sign of this that if afterward it were to become know that he was not baptized, then, if he deceived them he will be expelled from the congregation and not received again unless, after doing penance, he will be baptized. On the other hand, if it is not his fault, he would not be cast out, rather what he lacked will be perfected in him. It would not be judged that he was not in the Church, but will be judged to have entered through another way than the ordinary power. For this very reason, Innocent III,[25] judged that a priest who was not baptized was truly in the Church, and commanded sacrifice to be offered for his soul just as for the faithful. Dionysius of Alexandria, as we have it in

---

[25] cap. Apostolicam, de Presbytero non Baptizato.

church history,[26] judged that a certain man was truly in the Church whom it was certain was not truly baptized but only secured the other Sacraments as one of the baptized.

*Resp. b)* Two things can be considered on Bishops: Firstly, that they hold the place of Christ so for that reason we owe obedience to them, and because they cannot deceive us in those things necessary for salvation. Secondly, that they might have the power of Order and Jurisdiction. If it is considered in the first mode, we are certain with an infallible certitude that these, whom we see, are our true Bishops and Pastors. For this, neither faith, nor the character of order, nor even legitimate election is required, but only that they be held for such by the Church. Since they are Bishops on account of the Church, they are not against it; God assists those who are held for such lest they would err in teaching the Church. Now, if this is considered in the second manner, we do not have any but a moral certitude that these will truly be Bishops, although it is certain, with infallible certitude, that at least some are true, otherwise God will have deserted the Church. For this purpose, to hold the Church is certain and clearly visible in so far as the heads and members, the first consideration suffices.

*Resp. c)* The secret excommunicates are in the Church by number but not by merit, *de facto* not *de jure.*

*Resp. d)* In the first place, I say the difficulty is that men of this sort are not detected on the spot, but

---

[26] *Hist. Eccles.*, lib. 7, cap. 8.

nevertheless delude the Church for a long time, still nothing detrimental can happen from that. The Church does not number those among her own except by reason of external profession (they do not judge men regarding their internal life). Moreover, that external profession is very holy, although badly usurped by men such as these. Therefore, they are in the body of the Church while they are joined to the faithful in the bond of profession and obedience, because it binds the universal Church, and renders it into one body. Nevertheless, it does not follow that the Church on that account is the body of heretics, pagans and hypocrites, since even if a few men such as these are in the Church, nevertheless, we are certain with the certitude of divine faith that in the same Church, there are truly many faithful, pious and elect; just as in the human body nail and hair are discovered which do not live, and still no man thence gathers that the human body is nothing but nails and hair.

## CHAPTER XI
*Another Controversy is Proposed: Whether the Church is Always Visible, or Whether it can Err and Defect*

E HAVE explained what the Church is. Now we must speak about what kind of thing it is. There is conflict between us and the heretics on three matters. 1) They say the true Church is invisible and known only to God. Thus it is noted by Frederick Staphilus[1] that, in the beginning the Lutherans made the Church invisible, then at length, when they saw the absurdity which followed thence, by a secret counsel, they established that the Church may be said to be visible, but still by this name of visible they mean really invisible.

First of all, we take Luther in his work on *The Slave Will*. When Erasmus objected to him that it was not credible that God would desert the Church for so long a time, Luther responded that God never deserted the true Church, but that which is commonly called the Church is not the Church of Christ, *i.e.* the Pope, Bishops, clergy, monks and the remaining multitude of Catholics, rather it is a certain pious few whom, like a remnant, God preserves. And this was always in the world, that the Church that men said was the Church was not rather the certain pious and few. In another place he says the Church

---

[1] *Prima Apologia*, part. 3.

is spiritual and only perceptible by faith.[2] In another work he says the same thing, "Who will show us the Church since it is hidden in the spirit and only believed? In the same way as it is said, I believe in the holy Church?"[3]

Now the Centuriators of Magdeburg define the Church as a visible body,[4] nevertheless they distinguish two Churches, and say the true Church is for the most part scanty, while the false one is very numerous,[5] because only they pertain to the true Church who enter through the narrow gate, *i.e.* the truly pious, hence the true Church is invisible. They add that in the time of Christ, truly the Shepherds as well as the Magi, Zacharia, Simeon, Mary, and Anna, were in the Church but not the Priests and the Sadducees, because the former were pious, the latter were impious.[6]

Philip Melanchthon repeats as often as he can that the Church is visible.[7] Nevertheless, he says in the same place that the word of God must be followed in controversies according to the confession of the true Church. Moreover, this true Church he says cannot be Bishops and priests, nor a greater part of a Council, but certain pious and elect illuminated by God. Moreover, he says in the time of Elijah, the true Church was Elijah, Elisha, and the others

---

[2] lib. *contra Catharinum.*

[3] *De abroganda Missa privata,* pars 1.

[4] Cent. 1, lib. 1, ca. 4, col. 170.

[5] *Ibid.,* col. 178.

[6] *Ibid,* col. 181.

[7] *in locis,* locus 12.

that adhered to them, but not the remaining multitude of the Jews. Lastly, that in the time of Christ, the Church was Zachariah, Simeon, Mary and the shepherds because they were pious.

Brenz says in the Württemberg Confession[8] that the Church of God has the promise, still one must not stand before the judgment of Councils because few of the elect are there, and because often the greater part conquers the better part. And in his prolegomena he says: "You see that he [Pedro de Soto] makes the Church visible and perceptible in its corporeal senses. Therefore that article of the Creed will have to be blotted out, 'I believe in the holy Catholic Church,' and must be replaced with, *I see and perceive the holy Catholic Church.*'" In like manner, Calvin says, "Scripture speaks on the Church in two ways, on the one hand when it gives the name to the Church, it understands that which is really in the presence of God. ... It is necessary for us to believe the Church is invisible and visible only to the eyes of God."[9] and again, "Moreover, to embrace the unity of the Church in that way, there is no need to pick out the Church herself with the eyes, or to touch it with the hands."[10]

2) They teach that the visible Church so erred in faith and morals that it defected inwardly. Calvin says this in his preface to *The Institutes*: "But it is no small thing that they erred from the truth, while they did not recognize the

---

[8] cap. *de Conciliis.*

[9] *Institut.* lib. 4, cap. 1, §7.

[10] *Ibid.*, §3.

Church except that which they discerned with their physical eye.... They groan unless the Church is always shown with a finger.... Why don't we rather more permit God that, since he alone knows who are his own, he will, now and again, take the exterior notice of his Church from the sight of men."

3) They teach that the true Church, that is the invisible one, cannot indeed defect, nor err, in those matters which necessarily pertain to salvation; nevertheless it can err in other things. Calvin argues thus.[11] We assert the contrary and we will confirm each point with its own arguments.

---

[11] *Instit.* lib. 4, cap. 8, §13, and other places.

## CHAPTER XII

*The Church is Visible*

FIRST, that the true Church is visible can be proved from all the Scriptures where the term Church is discovered. A visible congregation is always meant by the term Church. Calvin could not, and did not, advance even one passage where the term is attributed to an invisible congregation. Certainly, when it is said in Numbers, "Why did you lead the Church of the Lord into the wilderness?"[1] the Church is called that people who had gone out from Egypt. Thus in Kings, Scripture manifestly speaks on the visible Church, when it says, "The king turned his face and blessed every Church of Israel; for every Church of Israel stood."[2] In Matthew 16:18, "Upon this rock I will build my Church," by the name of rock one either understands Christ, or the confession of faith as the heretics do, or Peter as we believe, the foundation of the Church is always something perceptible, as is clear, and consequently, the Church herself is perceptible, or visible. Even if now we see neither Christ nor Peter, still both had been put forth to be seen by corporeal senses, and now both are seen not in themselves but in a vicar, or in their successor, just as the King of Naples is not invisible when

---

[1] Numbers 20:4.

[2] 3 Kings [1 Kings] 8:14.

the king is away since he is seen in his viceroy. "Speak to the Church, if he will not hear the Church, etc."[3]

Certainly neither [foundation] can be saved if the Church were invisible, as Acts relates, "Attend to the whole flock over which the Holy Spirit has placed you as Bishops to rule the Church of God."[4] How could they rule a Church that they did not know? "These being removed from the Church passed into Phoenicia,"[5] and in the same chapter, "When they came to Jerusalem, they were received by the Church." "Paul went up and greeted the Church."[6] How do these agree with an invisible Church? Paul says that he persecuted the Church of God;[7] but it is known whom he persecuted from Acts 9:2. Next, he says, "I write these things to you, son Timothy, that you know how you ought to live in the house of God, which is the Church of the living God, etc."[8] But rightly he could not live in it unless he know what it might be.

Secondly, it is proven from other Scriptures where the Church is not named, but is clearly described. "He placed his tent in the sun."[9] St. Augustine explains that he placed his Church in the open, just as the sun which cannot be

---

[3] Matth. 18:17.

[4] Acts 20:28.

[5] Acts 15:3.

[6] Acts 18:22.

[7] 1 Corin. 15:9, Galat. 1:31, Philip. 3:6.

[8] 1 Tim. 3:14-15.

[9] Psalm 18[19]:6.

completely hidden, so neither can the Church be hidden.[10] Likewise in Isaiah 2:2, Daniel 2:35, and Micah 4:1, the Church is compared to a great and conspicuous mountain which can be in no wise hidden, according to the common exposition of Jerome on these citations, as well as Augustine.[11] Likewise in Matthew, "A city placed on a hill cannot be hidden."[12] Augustine explains that this is about the Church. Therefore, the gospel parables on the sand, the net and the sheepfold, the dinner party etc. all show that the true Church, which is the kingdom of heaven, is visible.[13]

Thirdly, it is proved from the very beginning and progress of the Church. So as to pass over the Old Testament we note that the Church was so visible that they carried the visible sign of circumcision in their flesh. In the New Testament the Christian Church was whole in the beginning in the Apostles and disciples of Christ, who were so visible that the Holy Spirit visibly descended over them on the day of Pentecost. Next, on one day three thousand men were added to them, and again five thousand by the confession of faith and Baptism, as is clear from Acts.[14] Thereafter, all these and only these were held to be in the Church of Christ, who had united themselves to those first through Baptism and Confession

---

[10] tract. 2 in epistola Ioannis.

[11] Tract 1 in epist. Ioannis.

[12] Matt. 5:14.

[13] *de Unitate Ecclesiae*, cap. 14, and other places.

[14] Acts 1-4.

of faith, and thence they did not receive through heresy or schism, or were expelled through excommunication.

Fourthly, it is proven from the very plan of the Church. The Church is a certain society, not of Angels, nor of souls, but of men. For a society of men cannot be spoken of unless it consists of external and visible signs, for it is not a society unless the members of that society recognize each other, *i.e.,* unless the bonds of society are external and visible. It is also confirmed from the custom of all human societies, for in the army, in a city, in a kingdom, and like things, men are ascribed to them in no other manner than with visible signs. For this reason St. Augustine says, " There can be no religious society, whether the religion be true or false, without some sacrament or visible symbol to serve as a bond of union."[15]

Fifthly, in the time of Christ, as Melanchthon and Illyricus would have it, the Church was only in Zacharia, Simeon, Anne, Mary and a few other pious persons, but not in the priests and the remaining multitude of the Jews. But it is certain that Zacharias, Simeon and the others communicated with the Priests in the temple, the sacrifices, etc. Zacharias was sacrificing in the same temple; Anna did not leave the temple; Mary went yearly to the temple; Christ himself sent lepers to the priests and said, "Do what they tell you." Therefore, the Lutherans actually act wrongly by not communicating with us and by not obeying the Pope.

---

[15] *Contra Faustum*, lib. 19, cap. 11.

THE CHURCH IS VISIBLE

Sixthly, it is proven from necessity; for we are all held to unite ourselves to the true Church and persevere in it under the danger of eternal death, *i.e.* to obey its head and communicate with the other members, as is clear from St. Cyprian,[16] Jerome,[17] and Augustine.[18] But this cannot be done if the Church is invisible.

Seventhly, from the aforesaid in the previous question, if the Church is a gathering of men using the same Sacraments and professing the faith of Christ, under the rule of legitimate pastors, as it was proved there, it necessarily follows that it is visible.

Finally, by the testimony of the Fathers, such as Origen, "The Church is full of brilliance from East to West, etc."[19] Cyprian, "The Church, imbued with the light of the Lord, sprinkles its rays throughout the whole world."[20] Chrysostom says, "It is easier for the sun to be extinguished than the Church hidden."[21] Augustine says, "There is no safety in unity except from the promises of God that were declared to the Church, that, being set up on a mountain (as it was said), cannot be hidden,"[22] and again, "Can we not show the Church with our finger,

---

[16] *de Simplicitate Praelatorum.*

[17] in epist. 1 ad Damasum de nomine Hypostasis.

[18] *de Baptismo,* lib. 4, cap. 1.

[19] Homil. 30 in Matthaeum.

[20] *de Unitate Ecclesiae.*

[21] Homil. IV, in cap. 6 Isaiae.

[22] *Contra epist. Parmeniani,* lib. 3, cap. 5.

brethren? Is it not clear?"[23] "What more is there to say than that they who do not see so great a mountain are blind? Who close their eyes to the lamp placed upon a lamp stand?"[24]

---

[23] Tract. 1 epistola Ioannis.

[24] *Ibid.*, Tract. 2.

CHAPTER XIII
*The Visible Church Cannot Defect*

OW it can be easily proven that this true and visible Church cannot defect. Moreover it must be observed that many waste their time when they try to show that the Church cannot defect absolutely, for Calvin and the other heretics concede that, but they say it ought to be understood about the invisible Church. Therefore, we mean to show the visible Church cannot defect, and by the name Church, we do not understand one thing or another, but the multitude gathered together, in which there are Prelates and subjects.

1) It is shown from the Scriptures where the Church is clearly named, "Upon this rock I will build my Church, and the gates of hell will not prevail against it."[1] What is said in 1 Timothy is similar to this, "That you might know how you ought to live in the house of God which is the Church of the living God, the pillar and firmament of truth."[2] In both it is a question of the visible Church, as we see and still hear the very truth asserted that the gates of hell are not going to prevail against that Church.

2) The promise is clear from other passages without the name *Church*, such as in the last chapter of Matthew: "Behold I am with you even to the consummation of the

---

[1] Matt. 16:18.

[2] I Tim. 3:15.

age." Such words were spoken to a visible Church, evidently to the Apostles and the remaining disciples, whom the Lord spoke to on the day of his ascension. And since these men were not going to remain in the body even to the end of the world, it was necessary to say this promise pertained to their successors. Therefore St. Leo I[3] and Leo II[4] understand this on the perpetual duration of the Church.

Moreover, in Ephesians we read, "And he gave some as Apostles, others Prophets, other Evangelists, others Pastors and Teachers to the consummation of the Saints in the work of ministry, in the building of the body of Christ until we all run in the unity of faith, and the recognition of the Son of God, in the completion of strength and the measure of the age of the fullness of Christ."[5] There the Apostle teaches that the ministry of pastors and teachers is going to remain in that Church for the continual building of the body of Christ, and hence the visible Church, even to the day of Judgment. Were there only an invisible Church in the world, that ministry could not be found which cannot be exercised unless shepherds and sheep recognize it. It must be noted that although the Fathers understand this passage on the spiritual measure of the mystical body, more recent authors understand it on the corporal measure of the body of the blessed which they say is going to be of such a magnitude, as things

---

[3] in epist. 31 ad Pulcheriam Augustam.

[4] in epistola ad Constantinum Augustum.

[5] Eph. 4:11.

were or had been in its perfect state of age. Nevertheless, all understand this passage on the last days, when the number of the elect will be filled.[6]

Besides, the Psalmist says, "God founded her in eternity,"[7] *i.e.* his Church, which is his city, as Augustine explains, and the matter speaks for itself, for the whole Psalm is on the foundation of the Christian Church, just as of a new and visible city. It begins, "The Lord is great and exceedingly praiseworthy, in the city of our God on his holy mountain: the whole world is founded in exaltation, etc." Likewise in Isaiah, "The Spirit of the Lord is upon me, ... and I will strike a perpetual covenant with them, and their seed will be known among the Nations, and their seed in the midst of the people. All who see them recognize them, because they are the seed which the Lord has blessed."[8] That this chapter is understood on the Church of the New Testament, Christ taught in Luke IV when he recited it in the Synagogue and explained it on his coming. Certainly this passage is so clear that it does not require exposition. How will that body be invisible if it is said, "All who saw them knew them because they are the seed which the Lord has blessed."

3) Next come the testimonies from parables in which the Church is meant by the consensus of all, for the sand in which there are grains and chaff; the net in which there

---

[6] See Augustine, *de Civitate Dei*, lib. 22, cap. 15, 17 et 18 where he touches on each explanation.

[7] Psalm 47[48]:9.

[8] Isaiah 61:8-9.

are good fish and bad; the field in which there is the grain and cockle; the dinner party in which there are the good and evil reclining; the sheepfold in which there are sheep and goats mean the visible Church, as even the heretics affirm. For an invisible Church does not have wicked and good, but only the good, according to their opinion. But the same parables teach that the Church visible Church is never going to perish even to the Day of Judgment. In Matthew it is said, "He will clean his field, and he will gather the wheat into his barn, but the chaff he will burn in the inextinguishable fire,"[9] which certainly will happen before the day of judgment. And again, "Permit each to rise even to the harvest. The harvest will be the end of the world ... Thus the angels will go out in the consummation of the age, and will separate the wicked from the midst of the just, etc."[10]

Fourthly, it is proven from the Scriptures, which speak on the reign of Christ. The Psalmist says, "His throne is as the sun in my sight, and just as the moon completed forever, and a faithful witness in the sky . . . and I will place his seed in age upon age and his thrown as a day of heaven."[11] "In the days of those kingdoms God will raise the kingdom of heaven which will never be destroyed: and his kingdom will be handed to another people."[12] "And for

---

[9] Matt. 3:12.

[10] Matt. 13:30.

[11] Psal. 88[89]:38.

[12] Daniel 2:35.

his kingdom there will be no end."[13] These passages cannot be understood except about the fact that the true and visible Church of Christ is not going perish. For the Kingdom of Christ, without a doubt, is his true Church. One cannot call a few secret men dispersed and separated from each other a kingdom, where one does not know the other such as the invisible Church of the Lutherans. For the kingdom is a multitude of men gathered who know one another.

Besides, in Psalm 88 [89] where the eternal kingdom of Christ is spoken of, it also says that in it there will be the good and the evil, and hence that the Church is visible, "But if its sons forsake my law and do not keep my justice, ... I will visit their iniquity with the rod and their sins with beatings, but I will not dispense my mercy from it, etc." St. Cyprian beautifully explains such a passage in *de Lapsis*. In the other verse in Daniel where it says the kingdom of Christ is perpetual, we also read that the kingdom is a great mountain filling all the earth, which Isaiah[14] and Micah[15] call a conspicuous mountain according to the Septuagint.

5) It is proven from the testimonies of the Fathers. Origen and Chrysostom affirm it in the places we cited, but Augustine and Bernard express it more clearly. St.

---

[13] Luke I.

[14] ὅὂέ ἔόὂάέ ἐί ὂάῖὂ ἐό÷Ϋὂάὲὸ ἡὶϓñάὲὸ ἐὶὂάί ἐὸ ὂὂ ὅñïὸ ἐõñßïὸ ἐάὶ ὁ ϊῖἐïὸ ὂϊὖ ἐάϊὖ ἐὂ' ἄἐñὺί ὂῶί ὂñϓῠί ἐάὶ ὺøὺὲ ἡόὰὂάέ ϋὂάñϋíὺ ὂῶί âïöí ῶί ἐάὶ ἥῖïõόέί ἐὂ áὺὂὂ ὂϋíὂά ὂὰ ἔὲíç . Isaiah 2:2

[15] Micah IV.

119

Augustine, disputing on Psal. 101 against the Donatists, (who said the whole visible Church had perished and only remained among the just in Africa) said, "But that Church, which was of all nations, no longer exists, it perished, yet those who are not in it say this. O impudent voice, just because you are not in it does not make it so. See to it lest you might were to be no more, since it will continue to be, even if you do not."[16] Further on, he introduces the Church speaking in this way: "How long will I be in this world? Tell me, on account of those who say the Church did exist but does so no longer, that it apostatized and perished from all nations; yea it announced and that voice was not empty. Who announced it to me, unless it was on the road? When did he announce it? Behold, I am with you even to the end of the age." He says similar things on Psalm 147 and in his work *On the Unity of the Church*, chapter 13, 20, and in other places.

The response cannot be made that Augustine speaks about the invisible Church since that does not perish nor is it going to, as the Donatists admitted, when they tried to apply the verse "I am with you even to the end of the age," to themselves, as Augustine related above.

On that verse in the Canticles, "I held him, nor will I let him go until I lead him into the house of my mother," St. Bernard explains, "Then and thereafter, the Christian race is not going to defect, not faith from the earth nor charity from the Church; the rivers came, the winds blew and dashed against her, and she did not fall, to the extent that

---

[16] In Psal. 101, sermon 2.

she was founded upon the rock, and the rock was Christ. Therefore, neither the verbosity of the philosophers nor the jeering of heretics nor the swords of persecutors could or will be able to separate her from the love of God."[17] These cannot be understood on the invisible Church, for the swords of tyrants will not pursue her, nor the verbosity of Philosophers or the jeering of heretics; therefore, the visible Church does not defect. Vincent of Lérin agrees, who rebukes the opinion of Nestorius as a grave error which taught the whole Church erred in the mystery of the Incarnation, to the extent that it followed blind teachers.[18]

Lastly, it is proved by natural reason. Firstly, if at some time only an invisible Church remained in the world, then at some point salvation would be impossible for those who are outside the Church. They cannot be saved unless they enter the Church, just as in the time of Noah they perished who were not added to the ark. Yet, they could not enter a Church which they were ignorant of, therefore they have no remedy.

Besides that, it is also shown from the plan of the one true Church that it is visible, therefore if the visible Church were to perish then no true Church would remain.

Next, either those hidden men who constituted an invisible Church openly profess their faith and abstain from the worship of idols or not; if they profess it, then the Church is not invisible, but particularly visible just as

---

[17] Serm. 79 in Cant.
[18] Commonitorium.

it was in the time of the Martyrs; if they do not profess it, then there is no Church since the Church is not the true Church if there are no good men in it who are saved. Moreover they are neither good nor saved who do not confess the faith, but instead, after they restrain it in their heart, profess treachery and idolatry outwardly, since in Romans the Apostle says, "For the man who believes in heart to justice, let confession be made by his mouth unto salvation,"[19] and again, "Everyone who denies me before men, I will deny him before my Father."[20] Consequently, it involves a contradiction for there to be a Church that altogether lacks a visible form, unless one were to place it outside the world where it will never be necessary to confess the faith.

---

[19] Romans 10.

[20] Matthew 10.

## CHAPTER XIV
### *The Church Cannot Err*

I T remains that we prove the Church cannot err in any way, not even by apostatizing from God. Still, first place must be given to a little more careful explanation of our adversaries teachings and our own.

Calvin says that the famous proposition, "The Church cannot err," is true with a two-fold restriction. 1) If the Church does not propose doctrines outside of Scripture, *i.e.* if it rejects traditions not written and only faithfully proposes what is contained in the Scriptures. Moreover, if you ask whether we might be certain that the Church always faithfully proposes those things that are in the Scriptures, Calvin responds by applying a second restriction, the Church always proposes faithfully what is contained in the Scriptures in matters necessary to salvation, still not in other matters and consequently some blemishes of error always remain in the Church.

The second restriction is that "The Church cannot err," is understood on the universal Church alone, it is not extended to the Bishops who are representatives of the Church, as it is said on the Catholic side. Every Bishop manages the person of his particular Church and therefore all Bishops manage the person of the whole Church. So Calvin holds of the greater institution,[1] while in the lesser

---

[1] *Instit.* lib. 4, cap. 8, §11, 12, 14, 15.

institution,[2] he fraudulently and mendaciously explains our opinion, saying we advance that the Church cannot err whether it uses the Word of God or not, since still he does not know we do not speak on the word of God absolutely, but only on the written word, and to say the Church cannot err whether it proposes that which is contained in the Scriptures, or doctrines outside of the Scriptures.

Next, our teaching is that the Church absolutely cannot err, neither in matters absolutely necessary, nor in others which must be believed or proposed that we must do, whether they are expressly held in the Scriptures or not, and when we say the Church cannot err, we understand that both on the universality of the faithful and on the universality of the Bishops, so that the sense might be of this proposition that the Church cannot err, *i.e.* that which all faithful hold as *de fide* is necessarily true and *de fide*, and likewise that which all Bishops teach as pertaining to the faith necessarily is true and *de fide*.

Since these have been explained this truth must be proved. 1) From the universal Church as it contains all the faithful and especially from that we read in 1 Timothy 3:15, "The Church of God is a pillar and firmament of truth." Calvin responds that the Church is called a pillar and firmament of truth because, like a most trusty guardian, it preserves the preaching of the written word of God, not because it cannot err in any matter.

---

[2] *ibid.*, cap.8, §146, 148, 149 et 150.

On the other hand, in this manner the offices of copyists were the pillars of truth because they very carefully safeguard all Scriptures, then the Apostle mentions Scriptures here, but he simply says the Church is the pillar and firmament of truth. Besides, how much more is a pillar than a simple guard? For the house rests upon the pillar and without that it falls. Thus when the Apostle calls the Church the pillar of truth, he means the truth of faith, in regard to us, rests upon the authority of the Church and the Church sanctions whatever is true and rejects whatever is false. Add that the Church was a pillar when there were no Scriptures, from which it follows that it is not called a pillar on account of protection of the Scriptures. Next, if it were a question of protection, then it would be better if Paul had compared the Church to a strong-box than to a pillar, for strong-boxes preserve books.

2) Besides, the Church is governed by Christ just as a spouse by her head, and by the Holy Spirit just as by the soul, which is clear from Ephesians, "He gave it a head over every Church, which is his body,"[3] and, "One body, one Spirit,"[4] and "A man is the head of a woman just as Christ is the head of the Church."[5] Therefore, if the Church could err in doctrines of faith or morals, error would be attributed to Christ and the Holy Spirit. For that

---

[3] Ephes. 1.
[4] Ephes. 4.
[5] Ephes.5.

reason, the Lord said, "The Spirit of truth will teach you all truth."[6]

Calvin responds that Christ and the Holy Spirit teach the Church all the truth that is simply necessary, but still some blemish is always left behind. It doesn't follow that error would be attributed to Christ or the Holy Spirit, just as ignorance, which is beyond doubt in the Church, is not attributed to them.

I respond: Just as a man who is head of a woman is not held to remove all ignorance from his wife, still he is held to remove all error from which some great evil might arise, although the wife may be excused by ignorance; so also Christ is held to remove all error from the Church, from which great evil arises, such is all error in regard to faith. For it is a great evil because the Church would worship God with a false faith, since divine worship consists in Faith, Hope and Charity, as Augustine teaches.[7]

3) We are obliged under the penalty of anathema to believe the Church in everything, as is clear from Scripture, "But if he will not listen to the Church, let him be to you as a heathen and a tax-collector."[8] Councils impose every anathema on those not assenting to the decrees of the Church, but it would be wicked to oblige under so grave a penalty to assent to uncertain and false matters.

---

[6] John 16.

[7] *Enchridium*, cap. 3.

[8] Matt. 18.

Calvin responds: Christ commanded that we listen to the Church because he knew the Church was going to teach nothing outside of the written word of God. On the other hand, so as to omit a great many things which we said in the disputation on traditions, the true Church teaches that the epistle to the Romans is the word of God, but the epistle to the Laodiceans is not, and likewise the about the Gospel of Mark and that of Nicodemus and other things that can be said, which were never written, consequently, it is not true that the Church teaches nothing outside the written word of God.

4) The Apostles' Creed teaches that the Church is holy and this holiness properly consists in the profession of doctrines, therefore, Christian profession contains nothing but what is holy, *i.e.* what is true in regard to a doctrine of faith and just in regard to precepts of morals, and in this it really excels all the professions of the Philosophers, Heathen, Jews and heretics. For all have some false doctrines mixed with true ones.

5) If Calvin's opinion were true, then a great part of dogmas of faith could be called into doubt, for there are many *de fide* teachings which are not absolutely necessary to salvation. Duly, to believe in the histories of the Old Testament, or that the Gospels of Mark and Luke are canonical writings, nay more any of the Scriptures, is not altogether necessary for salvation, since without this faith many were saved before the Scriptures were read; afterward, in the time of the New Testament, many barbarian nations were saved without them, as Irenaeus

writes.[9] But this is most absurd, nor would Calvin admit there can be any doubt about Scripture, therefore it is not true that the Church cannot err only in those matters necessary for salvation.

Lastly it is proven from the Fathers who, as we noted in the *Controversy on the Word of God*, on the question on the judge of controversies, all call upon the Church in whatever question of faith. Certainly they would not do this if they thought the Church could be deceived in some way. Tertullian says, "Well then, all Churches erred and the Holy Spirit looks to no one."[10] Augustine said, "We hold to the truth of the Scriptures since we do that which has already pleased the universal Church, which the authority of Scriptures itself commends, that because the Holy Scripture cannot be deceived, whoever fears to be deceived by the obscurity of this question, let him consult the Church about it, as Sacred Scripture points out without any ambiguity."[11] And again, "He speaks of the most insolent madness to dispute against that which the universal Church senses."[12]

Now that the Church also can not err representatively is proven first from the fact that if all Bishops would err, the whole Church would also err, because the people are held to follow their own pastors, by what the Lord says in

---

[9] lib. 3, cap. 4.

[10] *de Praescript.*

[11] *Contra Cresconium*, lib. 1, cap. 33.

[12] Epist. 118.

Luke, "He who hears you, hears me,"[13] and "Whatsoever they say, do."[14] Secondly, from the epistle of the Council of Ephesus to Nestorius, where Nestorius is compelled if he would satisfy the Church he could swear an oath to attest that he believes just as the Bishops of the East and West do. Likewise we see that St. Augustine calls the decree of a general Council the consensus of the universal Church,[15] and rightly so since the Church does not teach that it does not discern anything except through her pastors, just as any body you like through its head. For that reason, in Scripture a congregation of Priests and elders is called the assembly (*ecclesia*) of all Israel.[16] Chrysostom explains what verse of Matthew XVIII, "Speak to the Church," that is, to a Prelate. But this has more to do with the tract on Councils.

---

[13] Luke 10.

[14] Matth. 23.

[15] *de Baptismo*, lib. 1, cap. 18.

[16] 3 Kings 8.

## CHAPTER XV

*The Arguments with Which they Set up an Invisible Church
are Refuted*

T remains that we rebut the arguments of our adversaries. And the first is where they try to show that the Church is invisible by these testimonies. 1) "I will give my law in their hearts, and I will be their God, and they will be my people."[1] There, God distinguishes the Church of the New Testament from the Church of the Old Testament, which was an external body and for that reason had a written law on external tablets, e.g. stone; the Church of the New Testament, however is a people that has an interior law and for that reason it is written on their hearts. The same thing is contained in Luke, "The kingdom of God does not come with observation and they will not say, "look her, or look there. Behold, the kingdom of God is within you."[2] And in John, "The hour comes and now is when true worshipers will adore the Father in spirit and truth."[3] Therefore the Church of the New Testament does not consist in some exterior sign, nor is it bound to places and corporal ceremonies, just as we see in Hebrews, "For you have not come to an easy mountain or an accessible fire, but to Mount Zion, the city of the living

---

[1] Jeremiah 31:33.

[2] Luke 17:20.

[3] John 4:23.

God," etc.[4] There he compares the Synagogue to Mount Sinai, as well as the visible and tangible Church to the spiritual Mountain of Zion. Likewise in first Peter, "And you yourselves are built just as living stones of a spiritual house, a holy priesthood, offering spiritual sacrifices to God;"[5] But this house is the Church. At length that the Church exists is an article of faith, consequently the Church is not seen, but believed."

I respond: In the first passage from Jeremiah, it does not compare the Church with the Synagogue but the New Testament with the Old, which is clear in that passage. And although the New testament is properly charity, which is the law written on our hearts, the Old Testament is properly external doctrine, or the law written on stones, still it does not follow that the Church of the New Testament is invisible; just as the body of any animal you like is visible, still it has many internal parts which are not seen, such as the heart, the liver, the vitals of life, and like things; so also the visible Church has many invisible things, Faith, Hope and Charity, etc. and although these gifts are invisible, they are necessary in the Church and in the Church alone; still not in all its parts, just as a sense is necessarily in an animal and only in an animal, and nevertheless not in all its parts.

To the second I say the kingdom of God is understood in Luke by grace, through which God now reigns in the hearts of men, as Theophylactus explains it, or Christ

---

[4] Hebrews 12:18-22.

[5] 1 Peter 2:5.

himself as Bede explains it. For Christ speaks on both comings. The Pharisees asked, "When will the kingdom of God come," *i.e.*, the kingdom of the Messiah? But the Lord responded that the Messiah came and is going to come again on the Day of Judgment. Therefore, on the first coming he said, "The kingdom of God will not come with observation; behold the kingdom of God is within you," *i.e.* the Messiah has come and is present now. On the second he adds, "And they will say to you, behold he is here, or behold there, do not go out, just as lightening strikes under heaven, etc., so will be the coming of the son of man."

To the third I say, it is taught in that passage that the particular worship of God in the Church is going to be internal, but for that reason it does not follow that the Church herself is invisible, as we said above, nor does it follow that all external worship must be rejected and external temples be destroyed. The Lord does not treat on the place of prayer in that verse, but on the manner and rite. For if he meant to say that true worshipers are no longer going to worship God in Jerusalem or on Mount Gerizim, what he said would have been false. It is certain that Peter and John, after they received the Holy Spirit went up to the temple in Jerusalem at the ninth hour for prayer.[6] It is also certain that afterward there always were in Palestine Christians who worshiped God in Jerusalem and on mount Gerizim, and everywhere that bordered those places. He speaks on the rite of worship, or of

---

[6] Acts 3:1.

prayer, in other words, you will adore the Father neither on this mountain nor in Jerusalem, *i.e.* neither the rite of the Samaritans nor that of the Jews, but you will worship in the rite of Christians which is a rite worshiping in spirit and truth, but that is explained in two ways.

Chrysostom, Cyril, Euthymius oppose "in the spirit" in this passage to the ceremonies of the Jews, insofar as they were corporal, that "in truth", to the same ceremonies in so far as they were a figure and shadow of things to come. Theophylactus, St. Thomas and Cajetan oppose "in the Spirit" to the ritual of the Jews, which was especially external and corporal, but that, "In truth," to the ritual of the Samaritans, which was false and erroneous, for these worshiped the true God as well as false gods. Consequently, the Lord says that the rite of the Christian people will be particularly spiritual and at the same time true and pure from all error, although the spiritual rite will not exclude corporal ceremonies, in so far as they promote spiritual worship.

I answer the fourth with Chrysostom and Theophylictus, St. Thomas and others. Through the spiritual mountain of Zion and the city of the living God the Apostle does not understand the Church militant, but the Church triumphant, which is constituted from blessed souls. Accordingly, he compares the Synagogue with the Church and says the men of the Old Testament came to a physical mount Zion that they would see God there in some manner through corporeal images, but the men of the new Testament came not in fact but in hope, to the spiritual mount Zion, *i.e.* to the glory of the blessed, where

God is seen face to face, and it is added for this reason, "And the abundance of many thousands of Angels, and the spirits of the perfect just, etc."

I respond to the fifth that something can be said to be spiritual in two ways. In one way, according to substance, which is why in Ephesians they are called, "Spiritual wickedness in the heavens."[7] In the other way, according to the ordination to the Spirit, because something is ordered to the spirit or the spirit is dominated in it. This is why in 1 Corinthians 2:15 a man is called spiritual, and in 1 Cor. 15:44 the spiritual body, and in 1 Peter 2:5 all good works are called spiritual offerings, such as almsgiving and fasting. Therefore, St. Peter, when he says the Church is a spiritual house, he understands this in the second way, for he means the Church is not a house made from wood and stones, but built from men consecrated to God.

To the sixth it can be said that in the Creed it is not merely I believe in the Church, but, I believe in the holy Church. Consequently the holiness of the Church is without any doubt invisible. But it is better to say that in the Church something is seen and something is believed. For we see that body of men which is the Church, yet we do not see the fact that this body is the true Church of Christ, rather we believe it. For the true Church is that which professes the faith of Christ. Who clearly knows our faith is of Christ? We indeed believe it is firm and certain, but it is one thing to believe and another to see,

---

[7] Ephes. 6:12.

nay more to believe is the very thing defined by the Apostle, the argument is not of appearances.

What must be noted so as to understand it better, is that every teaching that is *de fide* is born from two propositions on faith and then the whole conclusion is not apparent; or one is on faith and the other is from what is apparent and then the conclusion is partly apparent, partly not apparent. Such is this conclusion, these men who now profess the faith under the Roman Pontiff are in the Church of Christ; for it arises from a syllogism: the Church of Christ is a body of men professing the faith of Christ, under the rule of the legitimate pastors; but these who are under the Roman Pontiff today are of such a body; therefore they are the Church of Christ. In such a syllogism, the major is on faith, and consequently is not apparent whereas the minor is evident, for we place nothing in the minor that is not perceived with the eyes or the ears. Therefore the conclusion is properly advanced as partly evident and partly non-apparent.

Next, the very matter, or (that we might speak logically) that *incomplexity*, concerning which the plan and definition of the Church is preached, is a certain visible thing; whereas the *complexity*, or the connection of what has been preached with the subject is preserved only by faith. The examples whereby this is illustrated are not lacking. Accordingly, that man who is Christ the son of God, the Apostles saw and at length that he was Christ the son of God they did not see, but they believed. For this reason in John 20:29, it was said to Thomas, "You have believed Thomas because you have seen me." And in the creed we say, "I believe in one Baptism," although we might see and perceive Baptism, *i.e.* the aspersion of water and the conferral of the words. Therefore we do not see, but we believe that the sprinkling of the water and the conferral of the words is the Baptism of Christ, that is a specific sacrament.

## CHAPTER XVI
*The Arguments Whereby our Adversaries try to Show the Church can Defect are Answered*

NOW, our adversaries attempt to show that the Church can defect and at some time did defect with these arguments. 1) In the beginning of the world Adam and Eve alone constituted the whole Church at least in power; but each lost the faith and apostatized from God, as is clear from Genesis 3 and from the Fathers.[1]

2) In the time of Moses the whole Church apostatized from God. For Aaron, the High priest, proposed to worship the calf, and the whole people shouted, "These are the gods of Israel."[2]

3) In the time of Elijah the whole visible Church had defected. For in 3 Kings Elijah says, "I alone am left. And the Lord said to him, 'I have reserved to myself seven thousand men in Israel who have not bent the knee to Baal',"[3] but these were secret not doubtful, since not even Elijah knew them.

4) It is said in Isaiah, "The ox knows its owner and the ass the trough of its lord, but Israel does not know me. From the soul of the foot even to the crown of the head

---

[1] Ambrose, lib. de Paradiso, cap. 6; Augustine, *Echirid.*, cap. 45 and Prosper, *lib. de gratia Dei*, contra collatorem.

[2] Exodus 32:4.

[3] 3 [1] Kings 19:10.

there is no health in it."[4] And in Jeremiah, "The houses of Israel have been confounded and their kings and princes, even the priests and prophets speaking in the wood; you are my Father, why do you contend with me in judgment? All have forsaken me, says the Lord."[5] And in Chronicles, "Many days will pass in Israel without the true God, without a priest or teacher, and without the law."[6]

5) It was foretold that the Church would be in visible inactivity. "The hosts will cease, and the sacrifice."[7] "When the son of man will come, do you think he will find faith on earth?"[8] "Unless the great dispersal will happen first, and the man of sin will have been revealed."[9] Therefore, Calvin thinks that what we read in Jeremiah has been said to us, "Do not trust in the words of the a lie, saying the Temple of the Lord, the temple of the Lord,"[10] namely these ancient Jews did not believe the prophets' warnings about the desolation because they saw the had the temple of the Lord, and external ceremonies; so Calvin thinks we boast that we have the ancient Churches, the successions of Bishops, the Apostolic See and meanwhile we do not attend to the Scriptures, which clearly foretell desolation to us.

---

[4] Isaiah 1:3.

[5] Jeremiah 2:26.

[6] 2 Chron. 15:3.

[7] Daniel 9:27.

[8] Luke 18:8.

[9] 2 Thess. 2:3.

[10] Jeremiah 7:4.

6) The General Council of Basel deposed Eugene as a heretic and all those adhering to him and chose Felix, thereupon after the Council was concluded and dispersed, again Eugene crept into the See without any canonical election and from him were born as many as were Popes, Cardinal and Bishops afterward, therefore at least from that time the Church adhering to the Roman Pontiff was not the true Church and since there was no other visible body, the visible Church perished. Calvin places this argument in the preface of his *Institutes* and again in the last place as though it were his strongest argument, adding, "This is discovered that it is necessary for them to adhere or to define the Church otherwise, or else we hold all to be schismatics."

7) They advance the testimony of the Fathers and first of all Hilary. "The love of walls gave you a beginning; you venerate the Church of God badly in buildings, you badly heaped under them the name of peace; to me mountains, lakes, prisons and deep holes are safer."[11] There he says the true Church was so obscured in his time that it could only be found in catacombs and caverns. Then Jerome, speaking in the same time, says, "The whole world groaned and marveled that it was Arian."[12] St. Basil says the same thing,[13] and St. Bernard,[14] so deplore the vices of the prelates of their times that they sufficiently show

---

[11] *Contra Auxentium.*

[12] *Contra Luciferianos.*

[13] epist. 69 et 70.

[14] Serm.33 *in Cantica.*

everyone had gone their own way and there was no visible Church. Then, Chrysostom teaches that sometimes there is no visible sign by which the true Church could be recognized, and therefore the only recourse is to return to the Scriptures.[15]

I respond, *ad* 1) If that our first parents sinned was for the Church to defect then not only the visible but even the invisible Church defected which is against our adversaries' point. Secondly I say there was no Church then, nor only two human beings in the Church, rather it was only the beginning of the Church and the beginning was both material and formal. Adam was the material beginning of the Church because he was the first of all in the Church; he was also the formal principle because he was the head or teacher and ruler of the people of God so long as he lived. Consequently the head of the Church cannot err by teaching false doctrine, nevertheless he can err by living badly and even by thinking badly as a private man. We see this happened in Adam since at one time he lived badly and perhaps even thought badly about God, nevertheless he did not teach badly.

*ad* 2) In regard to Aaron and the people that worshiped the golden calf, I say in that time there was neither a head nor a body of the Church to have defected since only Moses was the head whom it is certain did not err. Accordingly, Aaron was not yet the high priest since that happened later, as is clear from Exodus 40:12. Moreover the body did not fail, for all the Levites were immune from

---

[15] Hom. 49.

that sin, which is clear from the same chapter, where Moses said, "'If anyone is of the Lord let him join with me,' and all the sons of Levi gathered around him."[16]

*ad* 3) Concerning the time of Elijah, both the consequent and the antecedent of this argument are denied. The consequent because the plan for the Jewish people and the Christian people are not the same. The people of the Jews were not a universal Church as the Christian people are, but a particular one and on that account faithful and just men were found outside of that people, such as Melchisedech, Job and later Cornelius, the Centurion and the Eunuch of Queen Candice, as well as several others. Therefore, even if the whole Synagogue of the Jews defected all the Church of God on earth would not have defected on the spot. But the antecedent is also denied since it cannot be shown that the Synagogue of the Jews altogether defected even to the coming of Christ. After that it did not as much defect as it was changed into something better.

Now to that about Elijah I say that he did not speak on every people of the Jews, but only about the part that had been subjected to the king of Samaria. It is certain from the same book of Kings that in the time of Elijah Asa ruled in Jerusalem and after him Josaphat, the best kings, and under them the people and the priests very clearly persisted in true religion. Next, when the Lord said, "I have reserved to myself seven thousand men," he added, "in Israel." Then those who were under the king of

---

[16] Exodus 32.

Samaria were said to be of Israel, while those who were under the king of Jerusalem were said to be of Judah. Thus Philip Melanchthon was evidently deceived, since in his work he says that in the time of Elijah the Church was only in Elijah, Elisha and a few priests.[17] Calvin followed him in this error in the preface of his *Institutes*, which especially rests upon this argument on Elijah.

*ad* 4) Augustine responds to this when he taught that Prophets and Apostles sometimes rebuke the whole people as though not one of them were good, although there still might be many good and on the contrary sometimes they console all as if all were good when it is certain there are many wicked. Ezekiel says, "All the house of Israel is contrite on their forehead, and hard of heart."[18] Yet he also says, "The sign of the Thau is upon the foreheads of all that groan and weep, over all abominations that are done in its midst."[19] In Galatians the Apostle says, "O irrational Galatians, who bewitched you to not obey the truth?"[20] Yet he says later, "Brethren, and if a man be overtaken in any fault, you, who are spiritual, instruct such a one in the spirit of meekness."[21]

To the verse from Chronicles I respond that in the first place it is only understood on the kingdom of Israel, not the kingdom of Judah. Next, perhaps the Scripture speaks

---

[17] *in Locis communibus*, cap. de Ecclesia.

[18] Ezek. 3:7.

[19] *ibid.*, 9:14.

[20] Galat. 3:1.

[21] Galat. 6:1.

on the time that was going to be after the coming of the Messiah, for now many days have passed in Israel without God, without Priest and without the Law.

ad 5) I say that we do not boast in temples and the succession of Bishops and the Apostolic See in themselves, but on account of the promise of Christ who said, "You are Peter and upon this rock, ... and the gates of hell will not prevail." The Jews never had such a promise. Nor is it true that the ruin of the Church was foretold in the Scriptures, rather the opposite is true everywhere. Hence, to that passage of Daniel, even if Hilary, as well as even Hypolitus and Apollinarius who are cited by Jerome[22] understand that prophecy on the time of Antichrist, still it is beyond doubt that they were deceived. For Daniel speaks on the overturning of Jerusalem and the end of the sacrifice of the Jews. This is how Chrysostom and Theophylactus, and Jerome,[23] Augustine,[24] as well as Eusebius,[25] Clement of Alexandria,[26] Tertullian,[27] and the common opinion of the Jews as we also see cited by Jerome in his commentary on Daniel 9.

And the heretics are compelled to admit this answer; for they say that now is the times of Antichrist and has been for many centuries, and nevertheless the sacrifices

---

[22] in cap. 9 Danielis.

[23] in cap. 24, Matth.

[24] epist. 80 ad Esichium

[25] lib. 8 Evangel. demonstr. cap. 2.

[26] *Stromata*, lib. 2.

[27] *Contra Judaeos*, cap. 5.

and the sacrifice has not ceased, therefore they ought to understand this passage of Daniel not on the time of Antichrist but on the overturning of Jerusalem, which is evidently gathered from the Gospel. "When you will see the abomination of desolation which was spoken of by the Prophet Daniel, standing in the holy place, he who reads shall understand, then those who are in Judea should flee to the mountains.[28] Likewise he explained the same thing in Luke, "When you see Jerusalem surrounded by an army, then know that its destruction approaches, then those who are in Judea, let them flee to the mountains."[29]

Now, to that which we find later in Luke, "Do you think he will find faith on earth?"[30] I say that the Lord does not speak on faith simply, but on the outstanding faith that is found in only a few, and in the last days among very few. This is how Jerome explains it,[31] and Augustine,[32] or we could say with Theophylactus that the Lord speaks on faith absolutely and means few faithful are going to be left in the time of Antichrist, but still not be none, nor so few that they could not make the Church.

Now to that of Paul I say that by the name of dispersal either Antichrist himself is understood, as Chrysostom, Theodoret, Oecumenius, Theophylactus and Augustine[33]

[28] Matt. 24:15.

[29] Luke 21:20.

[30] Luke 20:8.

[31] *contra Luciferianos*

[32] *de Unitate Ecclesiae*, cap. 13.

[33] *de Civitate Dei*, lib. 20, cap. 19.

explain. They argue it should be called a dispersal as a metonym, because it will cause many to leave Christ; or it means the defection from the Roman Empire, as Ambrose, Sedulius and Primasius explain, which is a very probable opinion, or at length it will mean a going out from the Church that is not general but particular, *i.e.* not of all but of many, or at least of all secret heretics, as some of the Fathers beautifully explain it.[34] In the same way that many who were in the Church for a long time with a feigned spirit, at length clearly leave through the profession of manifest heresy, so when Antichrist comes nearly every secret heretic who then will be discovered in the Church will leave it, and join themselves to Antichrist.

ad 6) I say that the Council of Basel was at first legitimate, for even the legate of the Roman Pontiff was present, as well as a great number of Bishops, but in the time that it "deposed" Eugene and elected Felix, it was not a Council of the Church but a schismatic Council, seditious and of altogether no authority. Thus it is called in the last Lateran Council, sess. 11, and hence Eugene was always a true Pope and this clearly another lie of Calvin when he says that this Council preserved its authority and dignity even to the end.

In the first place, at the time the Council dared to pronounce sentence, there was no legate of the Pope present and all the Bishops had left, but a certain Cardinal from Arles usurped the office of president and because the Bishops were very few, they introduced into the Council a

---

[34] with Augustine, *de Civitate Dei*, lib. 20, cap. 19.

multitude of priests so that it became contrary to the form of ancient Councils, being composed not of Bishops but of priests.

Next, in the same time another Council was held in Florence in which the Supreme Pontiff presided and since the Latin and Greek Bishops who sat there without comparison many more than were at Basel, and together with the Bishops the Greek Emperor and the legate of the Latin Emperor were present, so that it could not be doubted which of the two was a true general Council of the Church.

Thirdly, God willed to show what he thought by afflicting Basel with a plague so horrible that a greater part of the Fathers who were there either were killed or were compelled to withdraw. Aeneas Sylvius (the future Pius II) related all of this in his history of the Council of Basel as well as what the heretics there had recently published as if favoring them on account of the condemnation of Eugene, when really he did them a great deal of harm. Add that the Council of Basel was continued at Lausanne and it subjected itself to Pope Nicholas V, as is clear from his epistle.

ad 7) Now we come to the citations of the Fathers. To the one from Hilary, firstly I respond in the way Augustine once did to the Donatists,[35] who objected with the same testimony, that the Church was at one time obscured by a multitude of scandals, still it stood out in its most loyal members, just as it did in the time which Hilary

---

[35] Epist. 48.

spoke. The Church stood out in Pope Julius I, Athanasius, Hilary, Eusebius Vercellensis, and then in Pope Damasus, Ambrose, Basil, Gregory Nazanzien and many others who were steadfast pillars of the Church.

Secondly, I say that Hilary spoke in that citation on the Church at Milan, in which many simple people venerated Auxentius as a Catholic even though he was still an Arian, since Auxentius behaved with such a wonderful subtly the Arians knew them as one of their own yet he was believed to be Catholic by man simple men. Hilary meant that no trust should be put in Auxentius even if he seemed to be a Bishop and preached in the Church and that it would be better to remain in prisons and caves with right faith than to be in the Church of God with heretics.

Nevertheless, what he said about one city, one Church and one Bishop cannot be applied to the universal Church. It can happen that one Bishop in one city and in one temple should teach heresy but still that all the Bishops in other cities and churches of the whole world would not do the same thing.

To that passage of Jerome I respond, there are two figures in his words, one of understanding, when he says, "The world groaned," for he calls the world a great part of the world, but not the whole world, the second of abuse, when he says, "and marveled to find itself Arian," for he calls the Arians improperly those who subscribe to heresy through ignorance. He speaks on that multitude of Bishops who throughout the world agreed with Ariminus and being deceived by the Arians decreed that the term όìïõôóéò (*homoousios, i.e.* consubstantial) must be abolished, even though they did not know what it meant. Certainly they were not heretics, nor did they err at least materially, just as if some Catholic might advance a blasphemous opinion externally with the tongue thinking it is a pious prayer, such a man would not properly be a blasphemer. For that reason the same Bishops, as they were admonished and recognized the fallacy, immediately corrected their error and with tears did penance for the blasphemy, even though it was only advanced by the tongue, and it seemed the whole world marveled and groaned to find itself Arian.

To Basil I say that in those epistles he did not deplore the vices of Catholics but the misery of the Church on account of the infestation of heretics. What was said in that citation are against Bishops, not against Catholic Bishops as Brenzthought, but against Arian Bishops.

It is perfectly credible that Brenz erred from malice rather than ignorance. In the same place that he teaches that Catholic Bishops are not the true Church he relates from the history of Ruffinus about the holy monk Moses, who refused in any way to be ordained by the Bishop of Alexandria, who was the primary Patriarch of Alexandria after the Roman Pontiff.[36]

But in the same book and chapter, Ruffinus says that the Bishop of Alexandria was an Arian and savagely persecuted Catholics and for this reason Moses refused to be ordained by him in preference to a Catholic Bishop,

---

[36] Ruffinus, *hist. Ecclesiast.* cap. 6.

thus there is no reason with which one could excuse or cover-up the fraud and impudence of Brenz.

To the quote from Bernard I say that he rebukes the vices of morals, but not of doctrine, and for that reason believed that those wicked Bishops were not truly Bishops. He himself refuted the heretics who said that bad Bishops were not really Bishops from the Apostolic Institution.[37]

To the quote from Chrysostom the response is above, those words were taken from an incomplete work which either has an Arian heretic for an author or was corrupted by heretics.

---

[37] Serm. 66.

CHAPTER XVII

*The Arguments Whereby our Adversaries try to show that all Shepherds of the Church can Err at the Same Time.*

UR adversaries try to show that the Church, or at least all the shepherds of the Church could err at the same time. 1) Because in the time of the prophet Micah, all the Prophets (about 400 with the exception of him) erred, as is clear from the Kings,[1] hence the Church, which they followed as they ought, was deceived. Secondly, in Isaiah it says, "His watchmen are all blind, they know nothing."[2] Thirdly, in the Lord's passion the High priest along with all the priests and elders of the people condemned Christ to the penalty of death. In Mark 14:64 the whole people, seduced by the priests, cried out to Pilate, "Crucify him!" In Mark 15:13 we see that at the same time all the Apostles lost the faith, since the Lord, "Reproached them for their unbelief and hardness of heart, etc."[3] And in Matthew, "You will all be scandalized on my account."[4]

Add that there are also Catholics that say during in the Lord's passion the true faith only remained in the Blessed

---

[1] 3 Kings 22:23.

[2] Isaiah 56:10.

[3] Mark 16:14.

[4] Matthew 26:31.

Virgin Mary, consequently they believe this is signified by the one candle that is kept alight in the Night Office[5] during the Triduum such as Alexander Alensis,[6] and Juan Torquemada.[7] But these are light enough and will be refuted with little labor.

To the first I say, those four hundred prophets clearly were pseudoprophets, and it is not unknown that they were even counseled by Achab himself. For in the same book when King Josaphat said, "Is there not any prophet of the Lord by whom we might ask the Lord?" Achab responded, "One remains, but I hate him because he prophecies nothing but evil." Certainly if anyone now in the midst of Saxony would counsel four hundred Lutheran ministers about justifying faith, and afterwards one Catholic, it would be no wonder if the greater part would err. Still, besides the Lutheran ministers, because apart from Saxony and neighboring places, there are many others where the true faith is preached, so it does not follow that all the Jewish teachers in the time of Achab erred, even if the four hundred erred. The Prophets who were in Samaria erred, but besides these there were in

---

[5] This refers to *Tenebrae*, which was celebrated with mostly the same ceremonies from ancient times until 1962, and today in all Churches attached to the liturgical books of that year. In that office there are 15 candles, which are extinguished as the Psalms are changed until there is one left. –Translator's note.

[6] 3 parte q. ult. artic. 2.

[7] lib. 1 *de Ecclesia*, cap. 30, et lib. 3, cap. 61.

Judaea many other Prophets and (what is foremost) there were priests in Jerusalem, by whom they duly apply to respond to consult from the law of the Lord.

To the second I say the those words of the Prophets are figurative, and directed to all, but really they ought to be understood not on all, but on many, as we said above.

To the third I say the priests and the High Priests did not have the privilege to not err when teaching the people, even to the times of Christ, but with Christ present and teaching us their error was a little nuisance. Nay more, this seems to have been foretold by Jeremiah when he said, "The law will perish from the priest, the word from the profit and counsel from the wise."[8] However, on account of the honor of the priesthood God provided that the judgment of the high priest Caiaphas in some sense (though not from his intent) was true and just. It is said in John 11:51 that he was the priest for that year and he prophesied.

What attains to the people, who cried out, "Crucify him," I say that people was not all of the Jews, but only some and perhaps a lesser part, for in the city of Jerusalem there was also Nicodemus and Joseph of Arimathea, and many others who disapproved of this, and outside of Jerusalem in the rest of all Judaea, and there were many Jews dispersed throughout the world who knew nothing about the death of Christ, hence they remained in the true faith and religion.

---

[8] Jeremiah 18.

Now I will speak to what the what was said to the Apostles: First, it is clear the Apostles were not Bishops except by designation, rather they were only material parts of the Church which could err, nor did the Church consist in them alone, for the status of the Christian Church with the obligation to enter it began on the day of Pentecost, when after all the mysteries of the redemption were carried out the Apostles began to publically promulgate faith in Christ as well as Baptism in Jerusalem. Therefore, even if all the Apostles erred in the time of Christ's passion in regard to faith, their error caused no harm to the universal Church.

Secondly I say, it is not probable that the Apostles lost the faith, since we do not read that they were rebuked except on the faith of the resurrection, but they could not lose that when they did not have it, unless after the Lord rose, were Christ often to have preached to them beforehand that he was going to rise; nevertheless they thought he spoke figuratively and they did not understand, nor did they believe. Accordingly, when he said in Luke, "They will kill him and he will rise on the third day," Luke adds, "and they understood none of this, and the word was hidden from them and they did not understand what was said."[9] We also read in John 20:2 that Peter and John, after they heard from Mary Magdalene that the Lord's body was taken from the tomb, right away they ran to the tomb and after they saw the garments and the shroud they believed that the body of Christ was taken

---

[9] Luke 18:33.

by someone, "For they did not yet know the Scriptures that it was fitting or him to rise again from the dead," *i.e.* they believed he was taken by someone because they did not know he ought to rise again. Besides, in Luke it was said to Peter, "I have prayed for thee that thy faith shall not fail."[10] How believable will it be that on the same night the faith of Peter failed so that it would not remain in faith, since what did not remain in his mouth is certain. Next, Mary Magdalene burned with the greatest charity in that three day period, as is clear from John 19:25 and 20:1, but without faith there can be no charity, therefore the Magdalene did not lose faith in Christ, which she had beforehand, therefore it is not the case that faith only remained in the Blessed Virgin.

Now, to what is said in the last chapter in Mark, "He rebuked their unbelief," this does not mean they lost the faith that they had, but they were late to believe what they did not yet believe, which at least would have been some kind of sin, but not properly infidelity. Moreover, that of Matthew 26:31, "You will all suffer scandal on my account this night," means the sin the Apostles would commit in flight, fear and staggering, even in regard to the faith, due to the fact of the Lord's passion; still not every staggering is infidelity, but only deliberate staggering.

But I marvel at Juan Torquemada, who, on account of this very weak argument based on the candle, says it is against the faith of the universal Church to assert that faith did not remain only in the Blessed Virgin on the day

---

[10] Luke 22:32.

of the Lord's passion. Rupert says,[11] that the last candle is also customarily extinguished at that time, and he adds that on those three nights after all the lights are extinguished, a new fire is customarily lit from a stone, and through it all the lights which beforehand were extinguished are lit, which signifies the Prophets whom the Jews killed in different centuries, and brought darkness to the minds of those killing them. Through the last Christ is signified, whom they killed, giving birth to the worst darkness in themselves, but through the new light, which is struck from the stone after those three days the new light of Christians is signified, which arose from Christ the stone struck by the Jews in our minds.

But if custom were neglected, the ancient Churches shall bring the force into that use which we have now, the last candle is not extinguished; then the response can be made with Abulensis[12] that through that candle the Blessed Virgin is meant, in whom alone, it is piously believed, there was explicit faith in the resurrection in those three days. Still, it does not follow that there was error in others or infidelity, because they were not held to explicitly believe in the resurrection until after its legitimate promulgation and approval, and especially for those who were out of Jerusalem and had heard nothing about Christ, and there it seems dangerous to say that true faith only remained in the Blessed Virgin; both because if the Church would have perished then not one person

[11] lib. 5 *de divin. offic.*, cap. 26.

[12] *quest. 14 prologi in Matthaeum.*

could be said to be the Church, since the Church is the people and the kingdom of God; and because then they who were away from Jerusalem even to that time that they had the true faith, would soon have lost it without fault.

# FINIS

Made in the USA
Monee, IL
19 January 2021

58072871R00098